WRAP IT UP

WRAP IT UP

50 CREATIVE AND STYLISH
GIFT-WRAP IDEAS

SALLY WALTON

PHOTOGRAPHY BY MICHELLE GARRETT

LORENZ BOOKS
NEW YORK • LONDON • SYDNEY • BATH

For Douglas and Pauline

PUBLISHER'S NOTE
Gift-wrapping is great fun, but some points should be remembered
for safety and care of the environment.

- Always choose non-toxic materials wherever possible, for example:
paint, glue and varnishes. Where these are not suitable, use
materials in a well-ventilated area and always follow
manufacturer's instructions.

- Needles, scissors and all sharp tools should be handled with care.
Always use a cutting board or mat to avoid damage to surfaces
(it is also safer to cut into a firm, hard surface).

- Protect surfaces from paint and glue splashes by laying down
old newspapers.

SOME USEFUL TERMS
UK: card, kitchen towel, PVA glue, adhesive tape
US: cardboard, paper towel, white glue, cellophane tape

Paperback edition first published in 1998 by Lorenz Books

Lorenz Books is an imprint of
Anness Publishing Limited
Hermes House, 88-89 Blackfriars Road
London SE1 8HA

© Anness Publishing Limited 1995

This edition published in the USA by Lorenz Books
Anness Publishing Inc., 27 West 20th Street, New York, NY 10011;
(800) 354-9657

A CIP catalogue record for this book is
available from the British Library

ISBN 1-85967-741-X

Publisher: Joanna Lorenz
Editorial Manager: Helen Sudell
Designer: Lilian Lindblom
Photographer: Michelle Garrett

Printed and bound in the United States

1 3 5 7 9 10 8 6 4 2

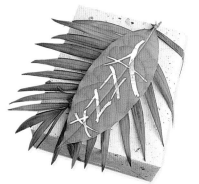

CONTENTS

INTRODUCTION

Successful gift-wrapping should both conceal and enhance your gift at the same time, adding mystery, excitement and an irresistible temptation to open up and see what is inside.

We have all hastily bundled a gift into inappropriate paper at some time and still found that the present was appreciated, but taking time to think creatively about gift-wrapping can be so much more fun. Gift-wrapping provides an opportunity to enjoy using paper in a huge range of colours and textures, mixed with ribbon, string, flowers and decorations – turning something ordinary into something spectacular.

There are 50 ideas in this book to inspire a more creative approach, and plenty of practical advice on how to achieve the most stylish results.

The wrapping should suit the gift, not overpower it, so try to resist spending more on the trimmings than the present inside. It is quite easy to get carried away and make a fabulously ornate parcel that is all but impossible to open because of an over-abundance of ribbons and bows! Gift opening should be exciting, not frustrating.

A beautifully-wrapped gift shows that time, thought and great care have been taken to offer someone a bit of extra happiness. And the bonus is the pleasure you gain from being generous and creative at the same time.

Papers

Paper comes in many different weights, textures, patterns and colours. Occasionally there will be an ideal gift-wrap for your present, but it is often more fun to customize your own plain paper.

First, explore paper sources: art and hobby shops, local printers, office stationers and the real specialists dealing in handmade and marbled papers. It is sometimes worth buying a single sheet of exquisite and expensive handmade paper to wrap a very special gift, but never discard the scraps; use small pieces mounted on plain card (cardboard) to make gift tags and labels. A handmade tag can be teamed with inexpensive paper to add a touch of class, but never feel tempted to do things the other way around – adding a cheap unmatching gift tag will instantly downgrade even the most luxurious of handmade papers.

Beautiful gift-wrapping doesn't have to be expensive, just imaginative. Tissue paper comes in a glorious range of vibrant colours, as does crêpe paper and cellophane (plastic wrap). Corrugated card (cardboard) sold by the sheet is great for making your own gift boxes, and the colour range is growing all the time. Traditional brown parcel wrap (packaging paper) should not be overlooked and is particularly good for hand-printing and stencilling.

It is a good idea to set aside a drawer for gift-wrapping materials and to buy sheets of paper as you come across them. This way you will have a range of papers that you especially like, ready to be used at any time. Paper ranges change all the time so there is no guarantee that you will be able to find a particular design in the future – buy it while you can. Keep a supply of gift-wrapping paper and plain paper to decorate yourself. It certainly beats dashing around at the last minute trying to find the one you have in mind.

Dolls-house paper
Craft suppliers sell this paper printed with tiles, brickwork and checkerboard floors. It comes in large sheets and is inexpensive and fun.

Hand-printed paper
All you need is plain paper and a spark of inspiration – and you may never buy gift wrap again. Potato cuts, rubber stamps, stencils, rollers or brushstrokes will all produce unique patterned papers. Use lightweight paper like plain newsprint, light rice paper or printer's paper. The very best cheap paper is

brown parcel wrap (packaging paper); it has one matt surface, is strong, folds well and looks marvellous.

Natural papers
There are so many sorts of handmade paper being imported from the East, the selection is enormous. It is possible to buy paper made from banana skins or recycled Bombay newsprint inlaid with rose petals! The colours are often hotter and spicier than home-produced papers, so find a specialist paper outlet and indulge yourself.

Photocopied paper
A large-format photocopier will produce large sheets of black and white paper. Designs can be enlarged, reduced, reversed and even coloured on the machine. Find an image you like and adapt it to make a unique and stylish gift-wrapping paper.

Tissue and crêpe paper
These cheap papers are sold in stationery and arts and crafts shops. Tissue paper needs to be layered to build up intense colour and is especially good for pre-wrapping gifts. An air of luxury is imparted by the rustling tissue under the wrapping paper. Crêpe paper is thicker and crinkly and its one drawback is that adhesive (cellophane) tape does not stick to it very well.

Textiles and Ribbons

There are many types of fabric and ribbons that are suitable for gift-wrapping. Here is a brief description of the ones used for projects in this book. Once you have tried using fabric in this way, many more patterns, textures and styles will enter your repertoire.

Wire-ed[...]
ribbon

TEXTILES

Hessian (burlap)
This is also known as hopsack and can be bought from furnishing fabric stores. It has a distinctive aroma reminiscent of the garden shed and is great for wrapping presents for a keen gardener.

Muslin (cheesecloth)
This fabric is fine, see-through and very light. It is best used over a plain paper. Gather and pleat it to make the most of its transparency.

Net (tulle)
Net is fabulous over brightly-coloured tissue papers. It has connotations of wedding veils and ballet dancing, so it makes a good novelty gift-wrapping material.

Towelling
Not generally thought of as a gift-wrapping material, but suitable for baby presents, for holidays and bathroom accessories. It is readily available, cheap and ultimately useful.

RIBBONS

Grosgrain
A classy matt, ribbed ribbon that is fairly stiff. It looks understated and expensive. Because the ribbing runs across the width it is quite difficult to gather into tight bows.

Paper ribbon
This comes in a twisted rope and can be used like this or unravelled to give a broad crinkled ribbon. It makes good bows that hold their shape well.

Raffia
Buy gardening raffia in either green or natural buff from a garden supplier, and bright dyed raffia from an arts and crafts shop. Both sorts are versatile and can be tied, twisted, braided and shredded.

Rosettes
The most commonly available are made of shiny paper ribbon, but there are fancier net versions, like the ones in the picture opposite. These can be used to add a final flourish, or more surreptitiously to conceal smudges and rips!

Satin ribbon
This comes in a huge range of widths and colours. It is sometimes overprinted on one side, as with the burgundy and gold stars. Satin ribbon forms superb bows but is slippery to use.

Sheer ribbon
This organza ribbon makes wonderfully light bows and trimmings. The colour and pattern of the paper underneath shows through.

Wire-edged ribbon
The ribbon will lie flat on the gift but can be twisted and will hold its shape. It makes most impressive bows that will never flop.

aper ribbon

Net
(tulle)

Satin ribbon

Muslin
(cheesecloth)

Towelling

Hessian
(burlap)

Rosettes

Sheer ribbon

Raffia

Accessories and Equipment

Creative gift-wrapping involves more than a roll of adhesive (cellophane) tape and patterned paper. There are art materials, Christmas decorations, office supplies and many other bits and pieces to help the crafty gift-wrapper.

Adhesive (cellophane) tape
Clear adhesive tape is best used with a ribbon, cellophane (parcel wrap) or net (tulle) that will cover and disguise it. Double-sided adhesive tape allows you to join paper invisibly. Matt adhesive tape is more expensive than ordinary adhesive tape, but is less obvious on gift-wrap.

Felt-tipped pens
Use felt-tipped pens instead of paint for colouring photocopied gift-wrap.

Florist's wire
Very handy for tying on decorations and ideal for fastening loops of ribbon when making big bold bows.

Saucers and glass sheets
Mix runny paints in saucers and spread layers of thick paint on to a sheet of glass for potato and rubber-stamp printing.

Glue
PVA (white) glue is a thick white liquid that dries transparent. It will stick most surfaces together in a relatively short drying time. Glitter glue contains glitter in a glue base.

Hole punch
A multi-sized hole punch can be used to decorate cards and make holes. It is particularly useful for gift tags. An eyelet punch gives a good finish.

Hot glue gun
Indispensable once you have used one, the glue gun delivers a small amount of hot, melted glue at the squeeze of a trigger. The glue dries almost instantly and is very strong.

Paint
Use water-based paints such as acrylics, poster paints or even sample pots of household emulsion (latex) paint to decorate your paper.

Paintbrushes
One broad- and one fine-tipped paintbrush will be useful for mixing and painting striped papers.

Pattern wheel
A cheap dressmaker's tool that can be used to make pierced patterns on card.

Pencil
Pencils are handy for making erasable guidelines and marks.

Rubber stamp and inkpad
A huge selection of rubber stamps is now available and it only takes minutes to stamp a sheet of gift-wrap and co-ordinate tags and cards.

Ruler
A transparent plastic ruler is useful for scoring, measuring and folding paper.

Craft knife
These extremely sharp and effective cutting instruments should be used with care, and never by young children. They are invaluable for stencil and card cutting.

Scissors
A selection of scissors would include a large pair for cutting paper, a small, sharp pair for ribbons, string and tags and, for an instant decorative edge, a pair of pinking shears.

Sealing wax
Light the wick and drip the melted wax to seal knots and make decorative seals.

Small roller and tray
These are very quick and easy to use, ideal for making up batches of matching paper.

Sponges
Natural or synthetic sponges are great for printing your own paper. Small make-up sponges can be used for stencilling and give better results than a brush.

Felt-tipped pen

Florist's wire

Saucer

Ruler

ber stamp and
ad

Adhesive (cello-
phane) tape

Glue

Double-sided
adhesive (cellophane)
tape

Pencil

Paint

Stapler

Small roller

Paintbrushes

Glass sheet

Sponge

ng wax

Hot
glue gun

Scissors

Pattern wheel

Hole punch

Measuring and Cutting

1 Place the box on the wrapping paper and measure two-thirds of the box height to cover the flap.

2 Roll the box over the paper to ensure the box will be covered and allow 5 cm (2 inches) for the overlap.

3 Measure with a steel rule the other side of the box and lightly draw a cutting line with a pencil.

4 Carefully cut out the paper to the correct size. Try to cut in long, even strokes to avoid tearing the paper.

Wrapping Boxes

Use the box to measure the paper size. Allow two-thirds of the box height for the side flaps and 5 cm (2 in) for a flat overlap. A folded, tucked-in overlap will need an average of 10 cm (4 in) extra.

METHOD 1. This method of wrapping a box is used by professional gift-wrappers.

1 Place the box on the paper, making sure that the side flaps are the same size. Wrap the paper firmly around the near side of the box and secure it half-way across the top with tape.

2 Apply double-sided adhesive (cellophane) tape to the length of paper nearest you, turn the box around, pull the paper up to overlap, peel off the backing strip, and press down on top.

3 Fold down the top flap at one end and secure it to the box. Smooth the paper along the sides with two fingers and fold the side flaps around to cross over, leaving one flap to fold up.

4 Line the edges of the triangular flap with double-sided adhesive (cellophane) tape, peel off the backing and press firmly against the side.

METHOD 2. This requires a longer sheet of paper.

1 Wrap the sheet around the box, checking that the side flaps are equal. Hold the two edges of the paper above the box and fold over a 2.5 cm (1 in) seam twice, folding away from your body. (This will make the paper taut.) Crease along the seam, then run a length of double-sided adhesive (cellophane) tape along near the edge. Peel off the backing, tuck the paper fold in and press the seam firmly down on to the top of the box.

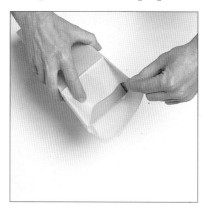

2 Fold the bottom flap up against the box, smooth the side flaps around with the flat of your hand and sharpen up the creases between your finger and thumb.

3 Fold up the seamed flap, leaving the sides until last.

4 Fold both side flaps across to meet in the middle, securing them neatly with pieces of double-sided adhesive (cellophane) tape.

Wrapping a Round Box

Many gifts come in round containers, for instance a tin of cookies or a selection of bath accessories. The shape need not be daunting at all, and will make a very neatly wrapped gift if you follow this method.

1 Place your gift upside-down in the middle of a sheet of wrapping paper. Make sure that your paper is big enough to reach the middle of the box when pulled up and across from any point around the edge.

2 Cut off the corners and, holding the box down firmly, pull up the paper and smooth it across the top, fastening it in the middle with a small piece of adhesive (cellophane) tape.

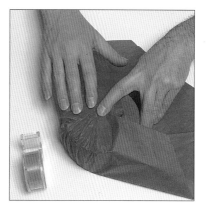

3 Pick up the remaining edges of the paper and pull them up, pleating the paper as you go, and tape them in the middle with the first corner edge.

4 Trim any excess paper away from the centre and tape in any loose edges. If you are tying a bow on top of the box it will cover the tape, if not, cut a circle of wrapping paper slightly smaller than the box and glue this down flat for a very neat finish.

Wrapping Unusual Shapes

Not all gifts come in convenient shapes and sizes for wrapping. While a stock of tubes and boxes may help wrap an awkward shaped gift, you may not always have a suitable container to hand.

Trimmings

The finishing touches to your present are all-important. The simple tying of an attractive bow can transform a gift. Here are just a few suggestions for completing your gift-wrap.

TYING A BASIC BOW

1 Decide on a surface that is going to be the base, in this case the teddy is able to sit up. Cut out a regular shape, either square, rectangular or round, from thick cardboard. Cover with a piece of your gift wrap.

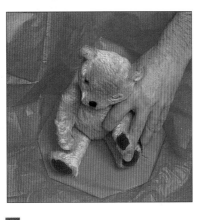

2 Place the cardboard in the middle of a large sheet of paper, or cross two lengths over for a larger gift.

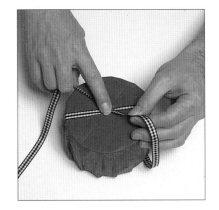

1 Pass the ribbon under the gift so that you have two ends of equal length. Tie the two together at the top.

2 Knot the tied ends so that both your hands are freed for tying the bow.

3 Pull up the paper from opposite sides and bunch it up on top of the gift. Tissue paper works well for this, because it creases in an attractive way. If you are using thicker paper, gather and pleat it as you make the bunch.

4 Tie a ribbon or cord firmly around the bunch, then arrange the paper into a balanced decorative shape. An ornament hanging down from the ribbon will help to draw attention back down to the gift.

3 Form two loops and tie together to make a simple bow.

4 Finish off the bow by cutting the ribbon ends into swallowtails. Fold the ribbon down the middle then cut from the fold towards the open edges at a slant. Make the cut towards the ends of the ribbon.

STRING AND RIBBON

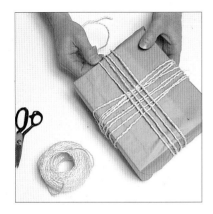

1 Wrap your gift in tissue paper then wind coarse string around the box at least four times in each direction.

2 Take a short, narrow red ribbon and use it to gather all the string together at the centre point. Tie a simple bow in the red ribbon and separate the strands of string out towards the edges of the box.

PINK AND GREY GIFT

1 Use a broad fancy ribbon on a plain background. Cross the ribbon over on top of the box then take the ends around underneath it.

2 Instead of tying the ribbon in a bow or knot, use double-sided adhesive (cellophane) tape to join it and give a taut, flat finish. The ribbon is shown off without the need for additional decoration.

PURPLE AND GOLD GIFT

1 Wrap a gift box in several layers of deep purple tissue paper, then surround it with a rope of gold.

2 Tie a double knot and let the tasselled ends fall across the gift as a decoration. Experiment with scarves, tie-backs and even pyjama cords (pajama belts)!

PINK ON PINK GIFT

1 Wrap the gift in pink tissue paper and tie it up with a pink spotted ribbon.

2 Thread a cookie cutter (this one is in the shape of a Christmas tree) on to the ribbon and tie a small bow. Christmas cookie cutters make great decorative tags, and with luck you may even get some cookies baked for you!

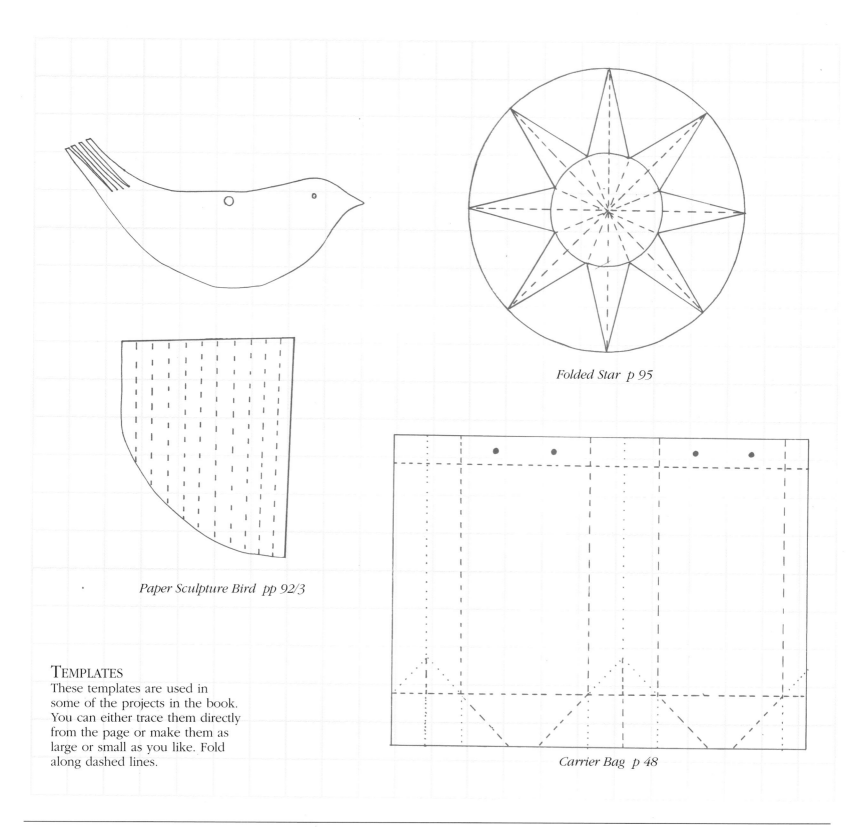

Folded Star p 95

Paper Sculpture Bird pp 92/3

TEMPLATES

These templates are used in some of the projects in the book. You can either trace them directly from the page or make them as large or small as you like. Fold along dashed lines.

Carrier Bag p 48

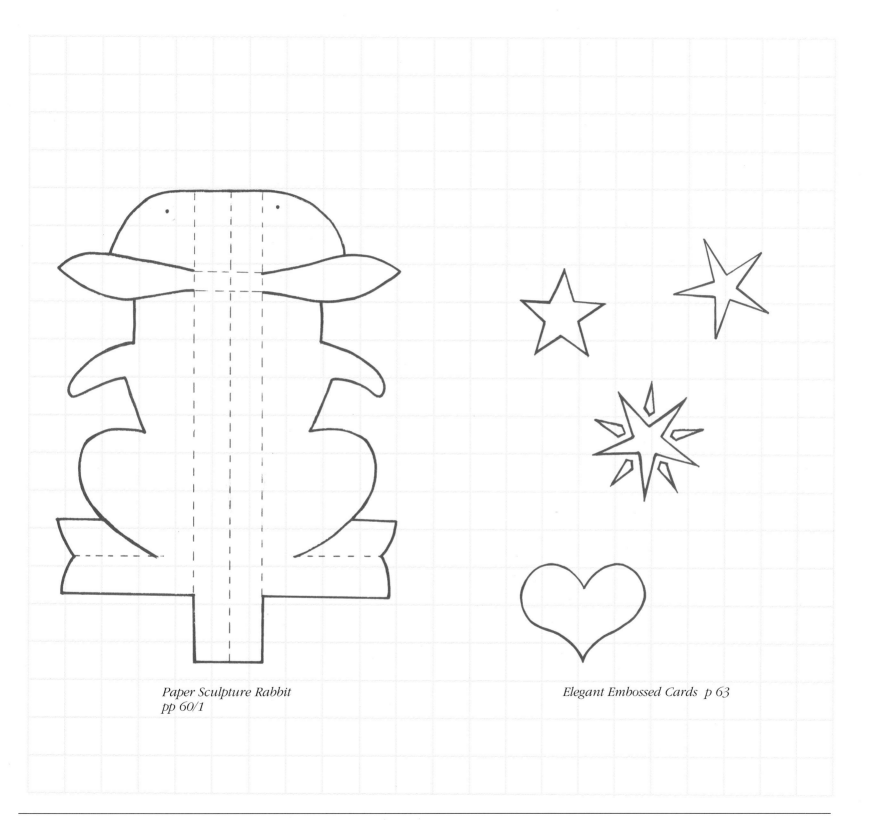

Paper Sculpture Rabbit
pp 60/1

Elegant Embossed Cards p 63

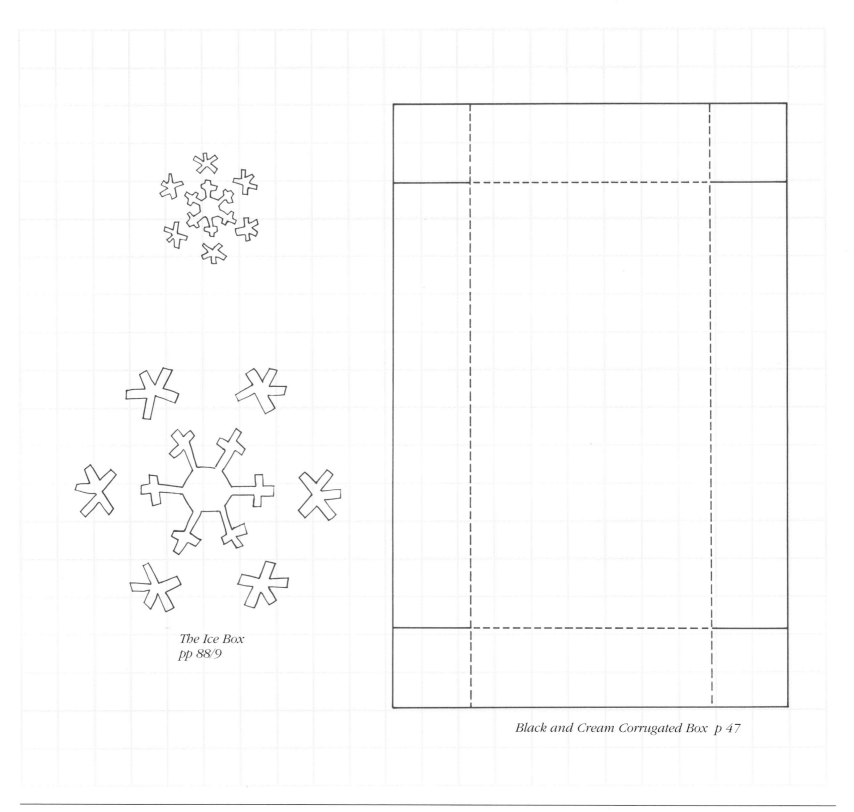

The Ice Box
pp 88/9

Black and Cream Corrugated Box p 47

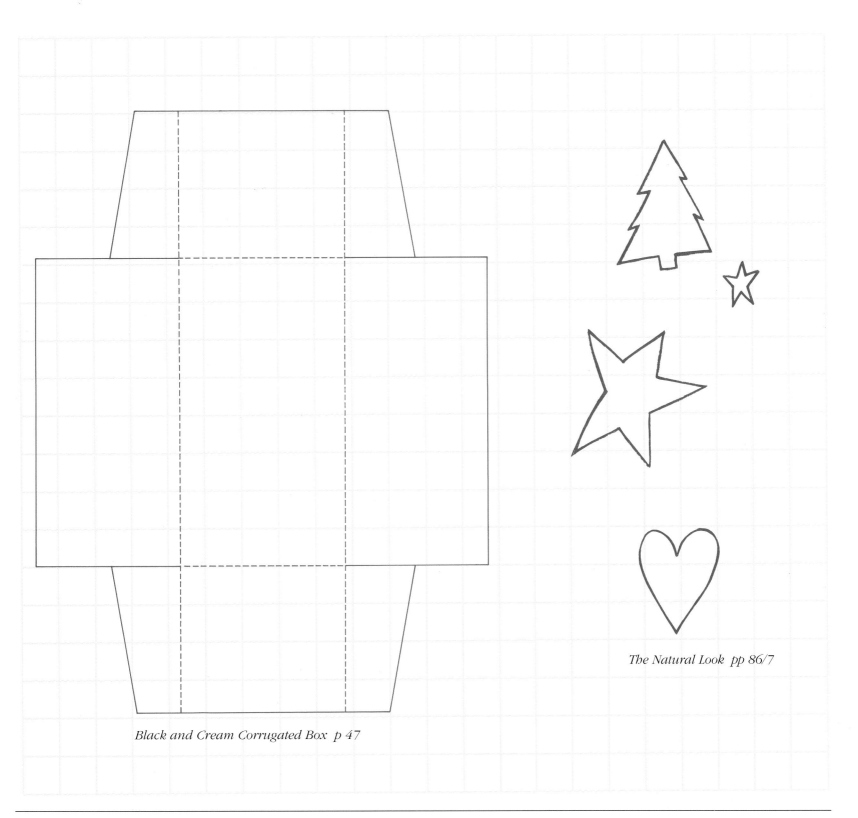

The Natural Look pp 86/7

Black and Cream Corrugated Box p 47

Greek-style Découpage

Découpage is the proper term for cutting out and gluing pictures on to an object for decoration. This paper features a Greek vase repeat pattern, but you could also use a mixture of different images, letter forms and numbers to make your personalized papers.

YOU WILL NEED
suitable black-and-white image
  to reproduce
scissors
paper glue
white paper, large and small
orange felt-tipped pen
adhesive (cellophane) tape
ribbon

ribbon

paper glue

black-and-white image

paper

orange felt-tipped pen

scissors

adhesive (cellophane) tape

1 Once you have chosen an image to reproduce, make 3 photocopies of it. Cut them out and stick them in a line on a sheet of paper. Make at least 10 photocopies of this sheet.

2 You now have 30 images to cut out and arrange on a larger sheet of white paper.

3 The first arrangement leaves a balancing white space as a background, with the urns spaced widely and inverted on the second row, moving up into the space left by the row above.

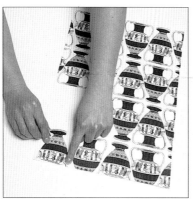

4 This arrangement allows less background space and the urns are used base to base and top to top. Cut some urns in half to fill the paper right up to the edges.

5 Photocopy your artwork on to the larger paper. You can also make reductions at this stage, returning to the smaller size for a small gift. Experiment with colour as a background, or leave the paper black-and-white.

6 Black-and-white paper contrasts brilliantly with this red moiré satin ribbon, set off with a generous bow.

Spring Meadow Stencil

In stencilling, a design is cut out of a sheet of card (cardboard) or other material. Paints or crayons are used to colour through the stencil leaving the design on the surface beneath.

YOU WILL NEED
pre-cut stencil
paper to decorate, handmade and/or textured but plain coloured
artist's sepia watercolour paint
saucer
small natural sponge (a make-up sponge is ideal)
kitchen (paper) towel
adhesive (cellophane) tape
ribbon
scissors

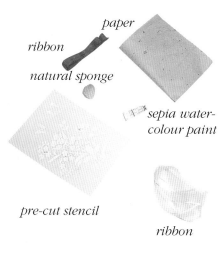

paper

ribbon

natural sponge

sepia water-colour paint

pre-cut stencil

ribbon

CRAFT TIP
There are many different pre-cut stencils available, mostly for the home-decorating market, but also in stationery and toy shops. You can also make your own stencils, by drawing or tracing then cutting a design from card (cardboard) or stenciller's plastic called mylar.

1 Position the stencil in one corner of the paper, lining up the edges. Dilute the paint slightly with a little water in the saucer and soak it up with the sponge. Dab the sponge on to kitchen (paper) towel to remove any excess paint, then begin to apply the stencil pattern, pressing lightly through the stencil.

2 Repeat the pattern across the paper, then position the stencil on the row below, between two above. This way the pattern will not divide up into blocks, but give a more all-over effect.

3 If there are any obvious blank spaces, fill them with random floral sprigs and butterflies.

4 Choose a complementary ribbon and finish the gift off with a simple bow.

Fishy Imprints

Rubber stamping is all the rage – it is a compulsive activity that gives instant, reliable results, and it is great fun! Check out local and mail-order suppliers to find the stamp image that is perfect for you. Ink pads come in a variety of colours.

YOU WILL NEED
rubber stamp
inked stamp pad
brown parcel wrap (packaging paper)
piece of 6 cm (2 in) square paper for measuring
double-sided adhesive (cellophane) tape
red raffia
scissors

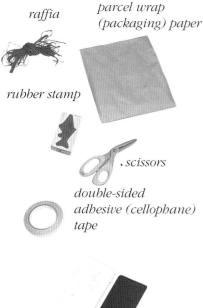

raffia

parcel wrap (packaging) paper

rubber stamp

scissors

double-sided adhesive (cellophane) tape

inked stamp pad

1 Press the stamp into the pad and test the coverage by stamping it on to scrap paper. Re-ink the stamp, and, positioning it in one corner and lining up the edges, make your first print.

2 Use the square of paper lined up with the fish's mouth and the edge of the stamp block to act as a positioning guide and make the next print. Continue along the length of the paper in this way.

3 Print another row of fishes at right angles to the first, filling the spaces between them. Continue stamping until the sheet is filled. Leave to dry.

4 Wrap the gift using tape. Tie strands of red raffia around the box and knot. Shred the ends and trim to a blunt shape with scissors.

Sponge-patterned Paper

Sponging is one of the most instantly effective ways of changing plain white paper into gorgeous gift-wrap.

YOU WILL NEED
saucers for the paint
acrylic paints – Indian red,
cobalt blue, viridian green
   and gold
sponge – synthetic or natural
kitchen (paper) towel
plain white paper
scissors
double-sided adhesive
   (cellophane) tape
broad satin ribbon

sponge

broad satin ribbon

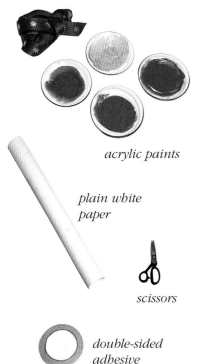

acrylic paints

plain white paper

scissors

double-sided adhesive (cellophane) tape

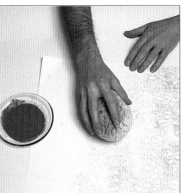

1 Fill a saucer with diluted Indian red paint. Dampen the sponge, squeeze it out then dip it into the paint. Print first on to kitchen (paper) towel then, beginning in one corner, lightly press the sponge on to the paper. Turn the sponge in your hand and make another print. Recharge the sponge as necessary.

4 Leave the paper to dry, wash out the sponge then print over the blue with green. The colour is denser than the red and gold. Experiment with different colours and try sponging on to coloured papers too; each printing will be different.

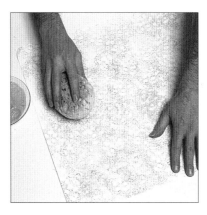

2 Leave the first printing to dry and wash the red out of the sponge. Fill a saucer with gold paint, dilute it then overprint the Indian red. The effect should be like soft marbelling. Try not to overdo the sponging; the gold will shine through as it dries and catch the light.

5 Leave the paper until it is bone dry then use it to wrap your present. Measure accurately to avoid bulky overlaps and use double-sided adhesive (cellophane) tape to secure the edges invisibly.

3 As a variation, use cobalt blue paint for the first print. This paper looks like the sea edge where the waves break and the water is foamy. Once again, use a light touch and rotate the sponge each time you print.

6 Because the pattern on this paper is so subtle you can afford to use a very bold colour co-ordinating ribbon like this broad satin burgundy ribbon with gold stars. (If you like, make a bow using florist's wire and cover the middle with a short length of ribbon, tying up the ends and tucking them under the bow. The bow is explained in more detail on pages 50 and 51)

Marbled Paper

Florentine marbled paper is the best in the world, so if your gift is precious and money is no object, invest in a sheet of this marvellous paper. Use expensive paper like this to wrap small boxes or books and keep the bows simple.

YOU WILL NEED
sheet of marbled paper
scissors
double-sided adhesive
  (cellophane) tape
narrow black satin ribbon

ribbon

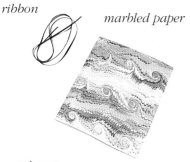

marbled paper

scissors

*double-sided
adhesive
(cellophane)
tape*

1 This is very precious paper, so measure accurately to avoid waste. You will need a 2.5 cm (1 in) overlap on the top, and side flaps two-thirds the height of the box or book.

2 Tuck one edge under the other and use double-sided adhesive (cellophane) tape along the edge nearest you, peeling off the backing and pulling the paper taut before pressing one edge down on to the slight overlap.

3 Fold down the top flap, smooth around the side flaps and sharpen their edges between finger and thumbnail. Place a small piece of double-sided adhesive (cellophane) tape at the apex of the bottom flap, then fold up and press it into the side.

4 Tie a fine black ribbon in a simple bow for the perfect, understated way to show off this exquisite paper. Bows and decorations should be kept simple so as not to detract from the impact of the beautiful paper.

Pretty Lace-effect Paper

This is a very quick and easy way to customize plain paper. All you need is a can of spray paint and a piece of old lace curtain.

YOU WILL NEED
backing board (back board)
lace curtain
masking tape
plain coloured paper
aerosol spray paint
scissors
adhesive (cellophane) tape
ribbon

ribbon

aerosol spray paint

adhesive (cellophane) tape

lace curtain

masking tape

scissors

plain coloured paper

CRAFT TIP
Shake the spray can for at least a minute before spraying on to a sheet of scrap paper. The spray should be even and very fine, with no variations or blobs – if these occur, just shake the can more vigorously for a little while longer.

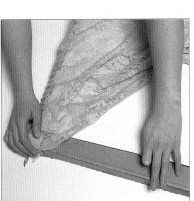

1 Use masking tape to stick one edge of the lace to a backing board. Slip a sheet of paper underneath it.

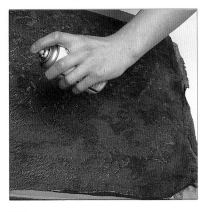

2 Follow the manufacturer's instructions on ventilation and agitation of the aerosol can. Spray on to the lace, moving your hand evenly across from left to right, and keeping the can at a constant angle of 90° to the lace.

3 Carefully lift the lace and remove the paper. Experiment on several sheets; it takes only seconds and is worth doing as results will vary.

4 Wrap the gift and trim it with a pretty ribbon. This one is transparent with wired edges which makes bow-tying effortless.

Checkerboard Potato Print

One potato has been cut in half to make this checkerboard pattern. One half is simply cut into a square, the other is given the same treatment, then a cross shape is made by cutting out four triangular sections and squaring off the ends.

YOU WILL NEED
chopping board
sharp knife or craft knife
potato
acrylic paints (or any water-based paint) in cobalt blue and cadmium yellow
2 saucers
kitchen (paper) towel
lightweight white paper
scissors
adhesive (cellophane) tape
blue ribbon

adhesive (cellophane) tape

lightweight white paper

acrylic paints

ribbon

scissors

potato chopping board knife

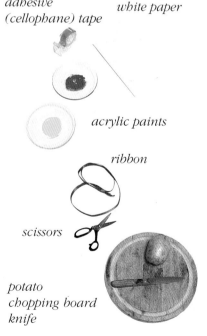

1 On the chopping board cut the potato in half with one smooth movement. Cut the sides off one half to make a plain square.

2 Cut the other half into a square, then cut out a cross shape by removing triangular sections around the edge and squaring off the ends of the cross.

3 Put the paints in separate saucers and have a kitchen (paper) towel handy. Print the yellow squares first, starting in one corner and working down and across the sheet.

4 Print the blue crosses in the white squares. Leave to dry.

5 Wrap the gift and use a thin blue satin ribbon, set off-centre as a trimming.

6 If you like, make a separate bow, securing loops of ribbon with florist's wire as shown on pages 50 and 51.

Antique Manuscript Gift-wrap

The ancient and modern are combined to make this unusual wrapping paper. A page from an old manuscript has been enlarged many times on a photocopier, to make a random pattern of white spaces and black shapes.

YOU WILL NEED
piece of old manuscript
plain paper
saucers
watercolour paints (yellow ochre and pink)
broad artist's brush
adhesive (cellophane) tape
scissors
ribbon

ribbon

artist's brush

scissors

adhesive (cellophane) tape

watercolour paint

old manuscript

VARIATION
Plain paper photocopy machines enable you to print on to a variety of different papers, although the black and white contrast is stark and interesting. Try a parchment yellow for a more authentically antique-looking paper which looks wonderful teamed with a rich velvet or moiré satin ribbon.

1 Photocopy a section of your chosen manuscript on to plain paper. Enlarge the copy by 200% and then make a copy of it onto larger paper.

2 Use diluted watercolours to tint the paper with streaks of yellow ochre and pink, giving it an antiqued effect. Leave to dry.

3 To wrap a round box, place it in the middle of the paper and begin pulling up the edges, sticking each section down with tape as you go. Cut a paper disc, slightly smaller than the box top and glue this on top to cover the gathered edges.

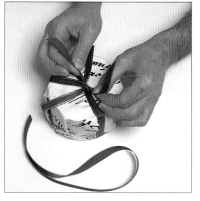

4 Cut three equal lengths of ribbon and tie them in simple knots on top of the box. Trim the ends of the ribbon to the same length.

Beautiful Blooms

The vibrancy of this floral paper gives any present wrapped with it maximum impact. You could make your own version if you have a favourite close-up colour photograph of flowers and access to a colour copier.

YOU WILL NEED
sheet of bold floral paper
double-sided adhesive
  (cellophane) tape
scissors
complementary ribbon

floral paper

ribbon

*double-sided
adhesive
(cellophane)
tape*

scissors

CRAFT TIP
Select one colour from the paper and match your ribbon to it. It would be best to place your gift in a box first, if it is an irregular shape, so that the pattern is shown off to best advantage on flat surfaces. Alternatively, fold a soft parcel into a square or rectangular shape which will have the same effect, making the most of the floral design without adding any distracting shapes.

1 Place your gift in a suitable box. Wrap the paper around the box, securing one edge to the box top with tape. Use double-sided adhesive (cellophane) tape along the other edge, pull taut and press down along the seam.

2 Fold down the top flaps, tuck in the side flaps, sharpening the edges with your finger and thumbnail. Check that the corners are sharp, fold up the bottom flap and secure it with double-sided adhesive (cellophane) tape.

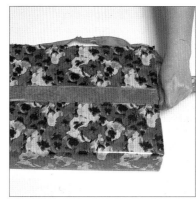

3 Measure a length of ribbon by taking it twice over and down the box in both directions. This is a Thai silk, wire-edged ribbon. Wrap it around the box, crossing underneath and tying on top.

4 Make a bow, starting with a single loop, taking the end around it and pulling through to make the second loop. Pull the ribbon into shape, trim and arrange the ends. The wire edging ensures the bow holds its shape.

Roller Plaids

This project borrows materials from the home decorator, using small paint rollers with emulsion (latex) paint to form the basic checkered pattern. The plaid effect is added in two stages, with drying time in between.

CRAFT TIP
The plaid pattern can be worked in all sorts of colour combinations, and will look particularly good in primary colours for Christmas gift wrap.

YOU WILL NEED
small paint roller, with integral paint tray
terracotta pink emulsion (latex) paint (sample-size pot)
white paper
1 cm (½ in) square-tipped soft artist's brush
olive green watercolour paint
saucers
No 3 soft artist's brush
white acrylic, poster or gouache paint
adhesive (cellophane) tape
scissors
red string

paint   *paint rollers and tray*

artist's brushes

scissors

adhesive (cellophane) tape

white paper

red string

1 Fill the plastic tray to about 0.5 cm (¼ in) with pink paint and coat the roller. Begin just in from the edge, and run parallel stripes down the length of the paper.

2 Leave to dry, then do the same horizontally. Leave to dry.

3 Put the olive green watercolour paint in a saucer and use the 1 cm (½ in) brush to draw stripes on the paper that cross through the centres of the white squares.

4 Dilute the white paint in a saucer and use the fine brush to draw lines that cross through the centres of the solid pink squares. Allow to dry.

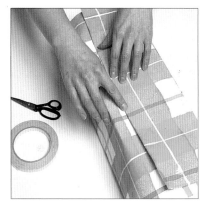

5 Place your gift on the paper and wrap it carefully.

6 Wrap the red string around the gift and tie it in a knot at the centre. Unravel the individual threads of the string to make an interesting crinkly bow.

Silky Sophistication

Sometimes a gift is best shown off by a mixture of purity and freshness, and this elegant wrapping achieves this beautifully. The fabric is pure white, and the fresh flower complements it perfectly.

VARIATION
If you like the idea of silk and fresh flowers but find white an unsuitable choice for your gift, try using hot pink silk with brilliant orange French marigolds for a startling clash of colour!

YOU WILL NEED
50 cm (20 in) white silk or
  lining fabric
scissors
Fraycheck or similar product to
  prevent edges fraying
double-sided adhesive
  (cellophane) tape
broad white satin ribbon
single perfect bloom (Madonna
  lily if possible)
pins
thin white satin ribbon

perfect bloom

broad ribbon

thin ribbon

silk or lining fabric

Fraycheck

scissors   *pins*   *double-sided adhesive (cellophane) tape*

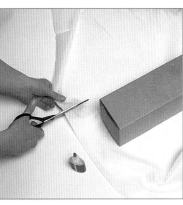

1 Use the box to estimate the size and then cut the fabric to fit. Seal the edges of the material with Fraycheck.

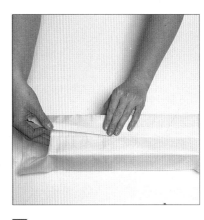

2 Stick one long edge of the fabric to the box top, then pull the other edge taut and fix it in place with double-sided adhesive (cellophane) tape.

3 Fold the top flap down, bring the side flaps around and stick the three parts together with a small piece of tape. Fold the bottom flap up to cover the tape, securing it with a small square of double-sided tape. The fabric should not be sharply creased, or it will resemble paper – gentle folds will enhance the fabric.

4 Run a length of broad white satin ribbon around the length of the box, to hide the seam. Cut it at an angle and stick the two ends together with double-sided tape, underneath the box.

5 Cut the stem of the bloom, so that the flower takes up two-thirds of the box's length. Use the pins to hold the flower in position.

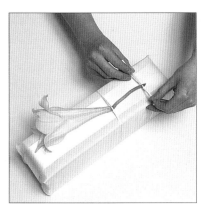

6 Use the narrow ribbon to encircle the box and bloom twice, tying knots and tucking the ends on the underside of the gift. Finally remove the pins.

Doubly Dainty Net Over Tissue

This gift is wrapped twice in very different materials. If your gift is not a regular shape then place it in a box, which could be square or round, and wrap the box in tissue paper.

The colours that are used in this project are pink and white, to give the effect of a ballet tutu, but these could be substituted for brighter contrasting colours, which would have more of a circus look.

YOU WILL NEED
pink tissue paper
adhesive (cellophane) tape
white net fabric (tulle)
pink satin ribbon
scissors

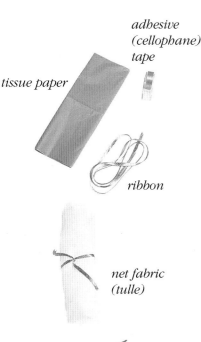

adhesive (cellophane) tape

tissue paper

ribbon

net fabric (tulle)

scissors

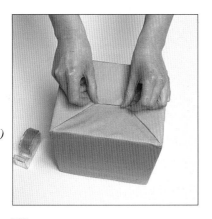

1 If possible use a cube or an up-ended rectangle to make the most of this idea. Wrap the box in pink tissue paper. Ordinary tape can be used as the net (tulle) will obscure it.

2 Place the box in the middle of a double layer of white net (tulle). The proportions will depend upon the size of the gift, this one used 2 metres (6 ft), trimmed down to a square.

3 Starting at one corner, pull up small sections of net (tulle), holding them in the centre of the box top with your spare hand. Work your way around the box like this.

4 Hold the bunch firmly, and arrange the folds and pleats around the box.

5 Take the satin ribbon up the sides of the box and twist it twice around the bunch of net (tulle), before tying a bow. Trim the ribbon ends. Tie a separate bow to attach, if you wish.

6 Froth out the net (tulle) on top of the box, trimming any extra-long edges, to make a full tutu shape.

Bundle of Joy

This project draws upon the old days, when infants were wrapped in elaborately folded squares of towelling, strategically held together by chunky pins. Wrap your gift in a layer of tissue paper first, before folding it up in towelling to make an unusual baby gift-wrap.

YOU WILL NEED
tissue paper
adhesive (cellophane) tape
scissors
50 cm (20 in) towelling (terry cloth)
2 nappy (diaper) pins
miniature pegs
thin elastic

tissue paper

elastic

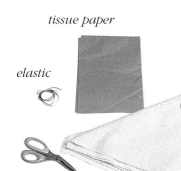

scissors

towelling (terry cloth)

adhesive (cellophane) tape

1 Wrap your gift in plain tissue paper using tape to secure the edges.

2 Trim the towelling (terry cloth) to a square and place the gift in the middle of it, with the points of the square shape forming a diamond. Fold the top triangle down over the gift and tuck the end underneath it.

3 Fold the side triangles around, gathering them slightly and tucking their points under. Fold up the last triangle and fold half of it under the sides. Secure at each side with a nappy (diaper) pin through the top and the side sections. Tie a length of thin elastic between the pins and attach a small square of paper cut into the shape of a wind-blown nappy (diaper) on the clothes line, to act as an original gift tag. Tiny clothes pegs add authenticity.

Neat Topknot

Butter muslin (cheesecloth) is soft, transparent and inexpensive. This project contrasts the hard-edged shape of a tissue-wrapped box with the soft, tactile quality of muslin.

YOU WILL NEED
tissue paper
scissors
adhesive (cellophane) tape
1 m (3 ft) natural or white
   butter muslin (cheesecloth)
gold tassled cord

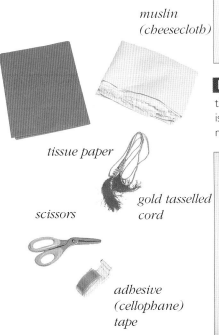

muslin (cheesecloth)

tissue paper

gold tasselled cord

scissors

adhesive (cellophane) tape

1 Wrap your boxed gift in coloured tissue paper. The muslin (cheesecloth) is transparent and the colour underneath adds another dimension.

2 Place the tissue-wrapped box in the middle of the muslin (cheesecloth) square. The fabric needs to be long enough to extend about 15 cm (6 in) beyond the central point of the box top. Gather up all the fabric, arranging the folds as you go, until you have a bunch in the centre of the box top.

VARIATION
Practise knotting a spare piece of muslin (cheesecloth) as there are many variations. A simple gathering up, twisting and tying will look beautiful.

3 Twist the bunch of fabric several times, turn it and tuck the ends under the rubber band. You may need several attempts until you achieve a satisfying result. Aim to have a neat chignon with no loose ends.

4 Tie a gold cord around the topknot, leaving the ends to dangle down. The parcel will look attractive and will be easy to undo. This is an ideal way to wrap irregular shapes.

Felt-covered Bijoux Box

Felt is a wonderful material to work with, it cuts easily, does not fray, can be glued to itself or most other surfaces and it comes in a brilliant array of colours. Pinking shears give felt an even, zig-zagged edge that looks really effective.

YOU WILL NEED
dark blue felt
hot pink felt
white dressmaker's chalk
scissors
PVA (white) glue
pinking shears
pencil
matching pink tassel
adhesive (cellophane) tape

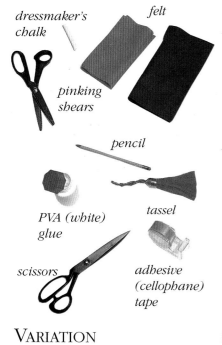

dressmaker's chalk

felt

pinking shears

pencil

PVA (white) glue

tassel

scissors

adhesive (cellophane) tape

VARIATION

This octagonal box has been covered with dark blue felt and decorated with a contrasting hot pink. You could use a round or square box to achieve a very similar effect. You could even make a box to cover.

1 You will need a box with an overlapping lid. Use your box as a cutting guide, marking the blue felt with chalk. You will need a base and sides which can be cut to actual size with no overlaps. Mark out three circles on the pink felt.

4 Cut out triangles of pink felt using the pinking shears, and place them along the edges of the box. If using a circular box, curve one of the edges. Cut two lengths of pink to finish off the lid and side of the box, using ordinary scissors on one edge and pinking shears on the other.

2 Spread the felt and the box with a layer of PVA (white) glue and stick the felt in position. The glue will dry transparent.

3 Cut out the felt for the lid with enough extra to cover the sides and fold up inside. Make notches where necessary to ensure a perfect fit. Spread with PVA (white) glue and stick down on to the lid. Dark-coloured felt seams are invisible when butted up closely against each other and glued in place.

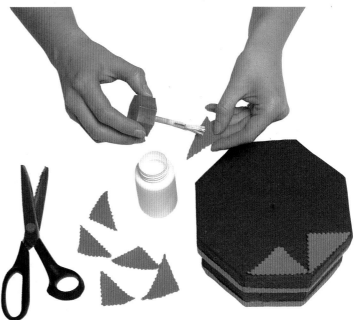

5 Cut out the three circles from the pink felt, using pinking shears for the largest one. Snip V shapes out of the circles, leaving the centres intact, to make petals. Glue them on top of each other with the smallest on top, make a hole through the middle and glue them to the centre point of the lid.

6 Using a sharp pencil, poke a hole through the lid and thread the tassel cord through the flower centre. Secure on the underside with tape and cover with a circle of felt.

Cross-stitched Gift

This unusual hessian (burlap) wrapping will turn your gift into a challenge and a conversation piece with the added novelty of the attached scissors that can be used to snip away the stitches and get down to the nitty-gritty.

YOU WILL NEED
50 cm (20 in) hessian (burlap)
ruler
scissors
adhesive (cellophane) tape
large-eyed needle
red tapestry wool
small scissors
plain black label
hot glue gun

1 Lay the boxed gift out on the hessian (burlap) and measure off five widths alongside each other. Allow 2.5 cm (1 in) for folding over at each end then cut the fabric to size.

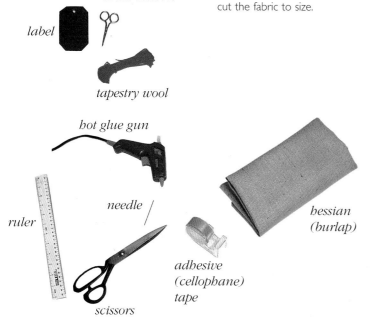

small scissors

label

tapestry wool

hot glue gun

needle

ruler

scissors

adhesive (cellophane) tape

hessian (burlap)

2 Score along all the fold lines using a ruler and the scissors. Fold the extra width in half to make a neat seam. Crease and fold up the hessian (burlap) around the box, temporarily holding the seams together with adhesive (cellophane) tape.

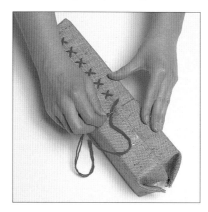

3 Start by securing the hessian (burlap) at the base with a single cross stitch that passes through the two opposite folds, then pass the needle under the fabric to emerge at the side seam. Sew cross-stitches up the sides.

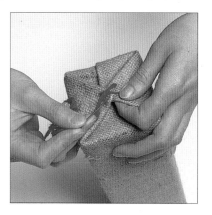

4 Finish off the top as you did the bottom, with a single cross stitch passing through the opposite folds.

CRAFT TIP

Hessian (burlap) can be scored like paper for accurate folding and its loose weave makes sewing it up very easy.

5 Attach the scissors to the label using a hot glue gun. If you don't have a glue gun use clear thread and a few strategically placed stitches.

6 Braid three strands of red wool and thread it through the label. The label should hang half-way down the box. Tie the end onto the cross stitch at the top of the box.

CONTAINERS & ADORNMENTS

Making Boxes

There is great satisfaction to be gained from making a three-dimensional container, and if you have cardboard, a ruler, a pair of compasses and a craft knife, you can make an assortment of attractive and useful boxes.

The two boxes described here are unusual and very different from one another. They are not boxes that you would cover with gift-wrap, simply place your gift inside them. The most important part of box making is accurate measuring, so double-check all your dimensions before you cut anything out.

FOR THE ROUND BOX
YOU WILL NEED
red, green and blue thin card
  (cardboard)
pair of compasses
scalpel
string
ruler
double-sided adhesive
  (cellophane) tape
PVA (white) glue
pinking shears
gold star

double-sided adhesive (cellophane) tape

PVA (white) glue

ruler

scalpel

star ★

thin card (cardboard)

pinking shears

compasses and pencil

1 Draw a circle on the green card (cardboard) using a pair of compasses. This will be the size of the box lid. Cut it out, then carefully measure around the edge using a length of string. Cut a strip of red card (cardboard) the same length, approx 5 cm (2 in) wide. Place a ruler lengthways along the strip, 2 cm (¾ in) in from one edge, so that 3 cm (1¼ in) remain exposed. Hold the ruler in place and cut notches at 1 cm (½ in) intervals along the length.

2 Join the edges of the red lid section with double-sided adhesive (cellophane) tape, then fold over the teeth and place the piece on a sheet of scrap paper. Coat the inside of the teeth with PVA (white) glue, move on to a clean sheet of paper and drop the green circle into position, on top of the red teeth. Press down firmly, then lift and leave to dry.

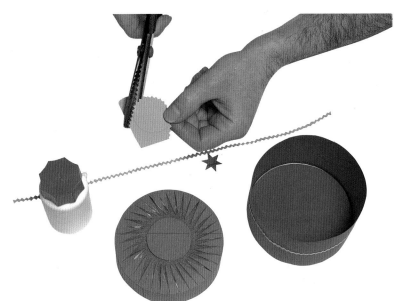

3 Make up the base of the box in the same way, but make the circumference slightly smaller to allow for the thickness of the lid. Make the sides at least 10 cm (4 in) high with an overlap of 3 cm (1¼ in) for the teeth. Trim the box with a strip of green card (cardboard) cut out with pinking shears. To finish off the lid, cut circles of red and green card (cardboard) to stick on top and glue a gold star in the middle.

VARIATION

The packaging industry has spent time and money perfecting the manufacture of efficient containers, so if you require a box to cover you could do no better than use a ready-made one from the pantry. If the size does not suit your gift then undo one of similar proportions and draw a pattern from it. This pattern can then be enlarged or reduced in size, to give you a perfect container.

FOR THE BLACK AND CREAM CORRUGATED BOX YOU WILL NEED

black and cream lightweight
 corrugated cardboard
ruler
pencil
craft knife or scalpel
double-sided adhesive
 (cellophane) tape or PVA
 (white) glue
eyelets and punch

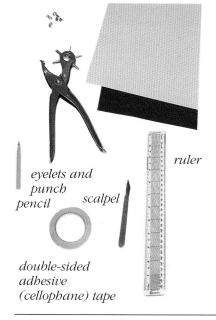

corrugated cardboard

eyelets and punch
pencil   *scalpel*
ruler

double-sided adhesive (cellophane) tape

I Using the craft knife or scalpel, cut out the lid and base following the enlarged pattern on pages 20 and 21. Score all the lines on the smooth side of the card.

2 Fold up the box and secure the sides with squares of double-sided adhesive (cellophane) tape, or a dab of PVA (white) glue. Fold down the sides of the lid and fix the flaps in position using an eyelet punch. Make sure that the eyelets are the same distance from the edge, so that they line up visually.

Making Bags

It is great fun to make paper bags and they can be used for all sorts of fun occasions such as children's parties, or to hold a slice of cake.

FOR THE CARRIER BAG
YOU WILL NEED
tracing paper
pencil
stiff (heavy) coloured paper
ruler
blunt knife
scissors
double-sided adhesive
  (cellophane) tape
hole punch
cord or ribbon for handles

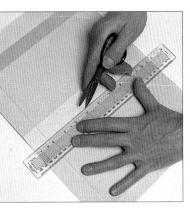

CRAFT TIP
There is a pattern on page 18 that will explain the various folds, and the process is easily mastered. Use stiff paper that is easy to score and fold for the best results.

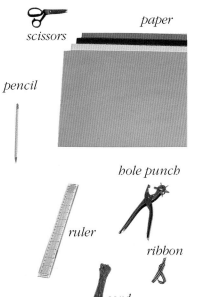

scissors

paper

pencil

hole punch

ruler

ribbon

cord

tracing paper

*double-sided adhesive
(cellophane) tape*

1 Enlarge the pattern from page 18 to the required size and transfer it on to stiff (heavy) paper. The dotted lines indicate mountain folds and the dashed lines are valley folds. Use a blunt knife or scissors and a ruler to score along the fold lines. Cut out the shape.

2 Stick the bag together using double-sided adhesive (cellophane) tape along the seams. Using the hole punch, make two sets of holes opposite each other on the top seam.

3 Place a square of double-sided adhesive (cellophane) tape below each hole made by the hole punch inside the top seam. Thread the ribbon or cord through the holes, peel the backing off the tape and press together to hold the handles in position between the bag and the overlapping seam.

FOR THE CRÊPE-PAPER BAGS
YOU WILL NEED
bright crêpe paper
pinking shears
sewing machine with zig zag
  attachment
contrasting thread
scissors
gold or silver cord
metallic stick-on stars

crêpe paper

stick-on stars

pinking shears

thread

scissors   *cord*

VARIATION
Use stickers of popular cartoon characters, animals, planes or cars to decorate gift bags for children's parties. Any motif can be used that suits the child's age or interests.

1 Decide on the bag size and, using the pinking shears, cut out a pair of rectangles from the crêpe paper.

2 Set a sewing machine to a large zig-zag stitch and use contrasting thread to sew along three edges of each pair.

3 Place the stick-on stars randomly over the bag, then fill with your gifts and tie up with the silver or gold cord.

Making Bows

Impressive bows are quite easy to tie – once you know how! You only have to watch a small child struggling with shoe-laces to realize how complicated it can seem to be – and explaining how it's done is even more confusing.

These two bows take a very different approach from shoe-lace tying, and both give spectacular results.

FOR THE POLKA-DOTTED BOW
YOU WILL NEED
box, wrapped in plain coloured
  paper
polka-dotted broad satin ribbon
scissors
fine florist's wire
double-sided adhesive
(cellophane) tape

1 Find the centre of a length of ribbon, wrap it around the box (this one is wrapped in recycled sky blue paper), crossing underneath and tying up in the centre of the box top. Take a second length of ribbon, form a single loop and pinch this between the finger and thumb of one hand. Use your other hand to make loops on either side of the centre, adding the end of each one to those being held.
It is important to keep the pressure constant, or the ribbon loops will slither out and you will have to start again.

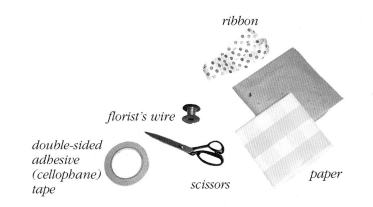

ribbon

florist's wire

double-sided adhesive (cellophane) tape

scissors

paper

CRAFT TIP
The polka-dotted bow is a billowing bow with plenty of loops and it looks especially good when made from broad satin ribbon.

2 Take a length of florist's wire and wind it around the pinched point several times, until it feels secure.

3 Finally cut a short length of ribbon and fold it in half lengthwise. Tie it across the middle to cover the wire and under the ribbon on the box. Separate the loops of the bow, pulling the ribbon upwards from the centre so that each section lifts and separates.

FOR THE GROSGRAIN BOW
YOU WILL NEED
box, wrapped in plaid paper
2 m (6½ ft) broad grosgrain
 ribbon
hot glue gun
scissors
double-sided adhesive
(cellophane) tape

ribbon

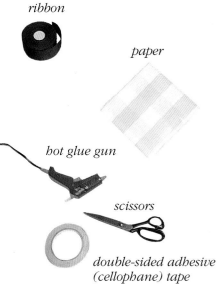

paper

hot glue gun

scissors

*double-sided adhesive
(cellophane) tape*

1 Wrap the ribbon lengthways around the box and apply a dab of glue from the gun to join the ribbon. Do not cut the long end off.

2 Make a long loop with the ribbon and bring it back to the middle. Add a dab of glue underneath and crease and fold the ribbon back to make a second shorter loop. Glue this in place too.

CRAFT TIP
Using a glue gun produces neater results and the material is more controllable.

3 Do this once more, making the last loop shorter still. Glue underneath, then take the ribbon over to the other side and repeat, to make three more loops. Finally, cut a short piece of ribbon and glue one end under the middle point, take it over the top and glue the other end underneath as well. (If you do not have a glue gun, use a needle and matching thread to secure the loops, working in the same order.)

Rubber Bands and Sealing Wax

Children love doing up parcels but their enthusiasm for the adhesive (cellophane) tape roll may leave you exasperated! Rubber bands are the perfect alternative to tape!

Sealing wax recalls the days when all parcel post had to have string and labels, and be sealed with irregular shapes of hard red wax.

FOR RUBBER BANDS
YOU WILL NEED
parcel wrap (packaging paper)
scissors
pack of coloured rubber bands
small folded card

FOR SEALING WAX
YOU WILL NEED
checkered paper
scissors
double-sided adhesive
  (cellophane) tape
coarse, thick string
sealing wax stick
cigarette lighter
gift tag

parcel wrap (packaging paper)

paper

gift tag

sealing wax

folded card

string

cigarette lighter

rubber bands

scissors

1 For the rubber bands, wrap the parcel, then stretch the bands length-ways and crossways to secure the flaps.

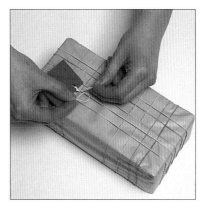

2 Add a criss-cross pattern in a sequence of colours. Loop a rubber band through the holes punched in the card, and tie it on to the gift.

3 For the sealing wax, wrap the gift with tape. Wind a long length of the string around the parcel three times. Loop the string around the three strands, knot it, then take it along the top of the parcel. Hold it in place, wrap the remaining string round three times, bringing the end up to loop around the crosspiece. Tie a knot.

4 Light the sealing wax wick and let the hot wax drip on to all the knots, then dip all the loose string ends in sealing wax. The hardened wax will hold the knots in place. Attach a gift tag to the string if you wish.

String and Raffia

Get down to your local hardware store or builder's supplier to unearth unusual gift-wrapping accessories. Garden twine, string, rope, hemp, jute, natural raffia, are all great for tying up packages, especially for rustic-looking gifts.

Coloured raffia can be bought from craft shops in a rainbow of dazzling shades. You can tease the raffia out, untwist it to make broad stripes, twist several strands together to make a broader rope or braid 3 different colours together.

FOR SIMPLE STRINGS
YOU WILL NEED
brick pattern doll's-house paper
scissors
adhesive (cellophane) tape
different types of string

FOR PLAIN AND
BRAIDED RAFFIA
YOU WILL NEED
coloured tissue paper
doll's-house checkered floor
    paper
scissors
adhesive (cellophane) tape
raffia, in natural (garden),
    yellow and orange
    (craft raffia)

1 For the simple strings, wrap your box in the doll's-house paper. Tie thin string around the box, and finish off with a simple shoe lace bow. Alternatively use coarse string and untwist the ends.

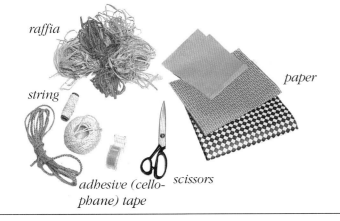

raffia

string

paper

adhesive (cello-phane) tape

scissors

2 For the braided raffia, wrap your box in tissue paper. Make two equal braids with raffia. Use two strands of each colour, knotting each end and leaving 5 cm (2 in) unbraided raffia beyond the knots. Take the braided raffia under the box then tie the two pieces together in a knot on the top. Shred the four ends to make tassels.

3 For the plain raffia, wrap your gift in checkered paper. Use several strands of natural raffia (more for a big box, fewer for a smaller one) around the gift and tie a big bow on the top. Tease out the raffia strands and trim any stray ends, but not too neatly, or you will spoil the character of the presentation.

Handmade Paper Folder

This handmade corrugated paper folder is a cross between a box and an envelope. It is a perfect way to wrap a silk scarf or lacy underwear. The gift can be folded up in coloured tissue paper first, to prevent it from slithering about.

YOU WILL NEED
tissue paper
scissors
adhesive (cellophane) tape
handmade corrugated paper
thick (heavy) coloured paper
4 eyelets and punch
length of fine string

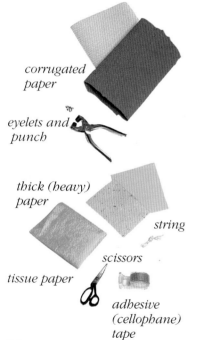

corrugated paper

eyelets and punch

thick (heavy) paper

string

tissue paper

scissors

adhesive (cellophane) tape

VARIATION
You can adapt this style of folder by using different types of card and fasteners. The nature and size of the gift will dictate the size of your folder.

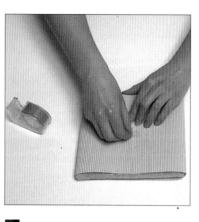

1 Wrap your gift in tissue paper and secure with adhesive (cellophane) tape. Measure the shape and cut a length of corrugated paper, just long enough to wrap around it. Secure with a small piece of tape.

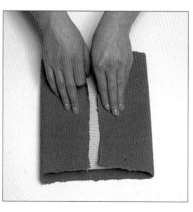

2 Turn the shape over and fold a second measured sheet around it to cover the open ends. There should be a small gap between the ends. If the paper has a rough or deckled edge, make use of it here for added interest.

3 Cut four 2 cm (¾ in) diameter discs and 4 contrasting 1.5 cm (½ in) discs from thick (heavy) coloured paper and fix them to the edges as shown. Use the eyelets to do this, or you could use brass paper fasteners instead.

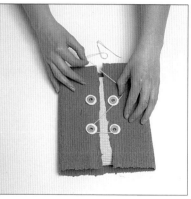

4 Wrap a piece of string around the discs, crossing over in the middle. Pull together firmly and knot to secure the folder.

Natural Garlands

The invention of the hot glue gun has revolution-ized garland making. All you have to do is just aim the preheated glue gun at the spot, pull the trigger to release a small amount of hot glue and press each piece lightly in position. The glue hardens in seconds and the bonding is permanent.

YOU WILL NEED

natural coloured handmade paper
scissors
double-sided adhesive (cellophane) tape
hot glue gun
length of broad grosgrain ribbon
selection of interesting dried natural decorations, such as small corn cobs, cinnamon sticks, bark, grasses and seedpods

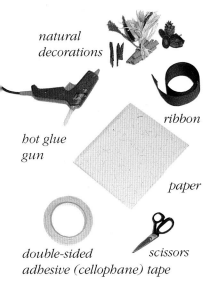

natural decorations

hot glue gun

ribbon

paper

double-sided adhesive (cellophane) tape

scissors

SAFETY NOTE

Take great care when using a glue gun as the glue is extremely hot and bonds in seconds.

1 Wrap up your box in handmade paper, using double-sided adhesive (cellophane) tape to secure the edges invisibly. Plug in the hot glue gun.

2 Wrap the ribbon lengthwise around the box, sticking the ends together with a dab of hot glue.

3 Begin making the arrangement by gluing the cinnamon sticks and bark along the ribbon. Work from the middle outwards.

4 Keep adding to your garland, building up the arrangement by adding similar objects on each side to make a balanced display.

Clever Fastenings

Sometimes it is fun to put aside the conventional gift-wrapping materials and experiment with unusual methods of fastening your presents. Look for alternatives in the hardware store or office stationers – particularly if they deal with the accounting or legal professions. They have all sorts of interesting seals, fixings and labels. Get a hot glue gun if you haven't yet succumbed, and use it to attach buttons, twigs or even bottle caps, then loop rubber bands around them to hold the paper in place.

These are just a few ideas to try, but you are bound to see other useful bits and pieces once you start to look in unusual places!

SAFETY NOTE
Take great care when using a glue gun as the glue is extremely hot and bonds in seconds.

Bamboo and raffia
Wrap your present oriental-style using a piece of bamboo as a toggle. Loop the raffia around either side of the box then tie a knot. Take the raffia under the box and loop it around the toggle. Tie it into the raffia strand underneath the box and trim the end off.

Buttons
Buttons are both decorative and functional. Use them in a row along the parcel seam, attached with a dab of glue from the hot glue gun. Then loop different coloured rubber bands around. Many different combinations are possible.

Decorative elastic
Use some coloured elastic with pendant decorations to secure the gift wrap around your parcel.

Doily hearts
The gift is wrapped in shocking pink-coated gift-wrap and the joining edges are covered and held together by two lacey paper heart doilies. Use glue or double-sided adhesive (cellophane) tape to hold them in place. Add a ribbon and bow as a finishing touch.

Eyelets and laces
You can use an eyelet punch, as shown here, or a hole punch with reinforcements to make a series of holes along opposite edges of the paper. Wrap the present in a contrasting colour tissue paper first, then cut your top sheet smaller than usual, so that a gap of colour shows from below. Thread a long shoe-lace through the holes and tie a bow.

Net (tulle) rosettes
Wrap a tube in pink tissue paper. Wrap a narrow pink ribbon around the tube and attach a rosette using a glue gun to conceal the ends. This is one for ballet girls and cheer leaders!

Safety pins
Wrap the gift in bright plain-coloured paper, then secure the end flaps and centre seam with different-sized safety pins. More pins can then be added for decorative effect.

Buttons

Eyelets and laces

Net (tulle) rosettes

Safety pins

Doily hearts

Bamboo and raffia

Decorative elastic

CARDS & TAGS

Recycled Look

There is a huge variety of rough-textured, hand-made papers and card (cardboard) around, many imported from the East and made from unusual exotic plants. Some have visible fibres, flowers or leaves and others are finer, with embossed textures applied to them.

YOU WILL NEED
corrugated black card (cardboard)
scissors
eyelets and punch
3 contrasting sheets of hand
  made textured paper
PVA (white) glue
raffia
selection of tissue paper scraps
hole punch
coarse string

hole punch

scissors

*card (card-
board) and
paper*

*eyelets
and
punch*

raffia

*PVA (white)
glue*

string

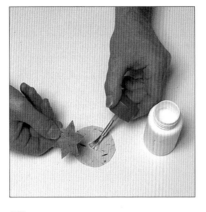

1 For a star tag, draw a star and cut the shape from tissue paper. Cut a handmade paper disc, spread it lightly with PVA (white) glue and press the star on to it.

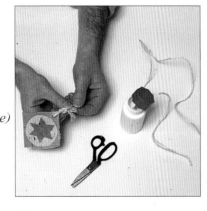

2 Cut a square to give a 1 cm (½ in) border to the disc, from contrasting handmade paper. Punch a hole in one corner and thread it with coarse string. Tie a knot and untwist the end to make a tassle.

3 To make a heart and bow, cut a rectangle from the black corrugated card (cardboard) and fix an eyelet in the centre at one end.

4 Cut a heart from textured paper, glue it, point down, at the other end of the rectangle. Thread some raffia through the eyelet and tie a bow that rests above the heart.

Pierced Patterns

These folk art-influenced labels have patterns pricked through, like the old tinware used in lamps and kitchen cupboards. A simple motif can be depicted on a piece of metallic or plain card (cardboard) by pricking out holes at regular distances apart, then the shape can be made ornate by adding different sized holes made with a hole punch or large needle.

YOU WILL NEED

scissors
metallic card (cardboard)
pair of compasses
dressmaker's pattern wheel,
   or selection of pins, needles
   and nails
hole punch
ribbon

hole punch

compasses

ribbon

scissors

*card
(cardboard)*

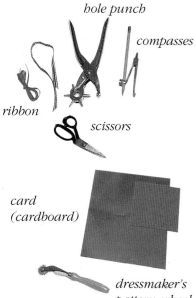

*dressmaker's
pattern wheel*

CRAFT TIP

A multi-sized hole punch is useful, but a series of different sized nails and pins will also produce interesting results.

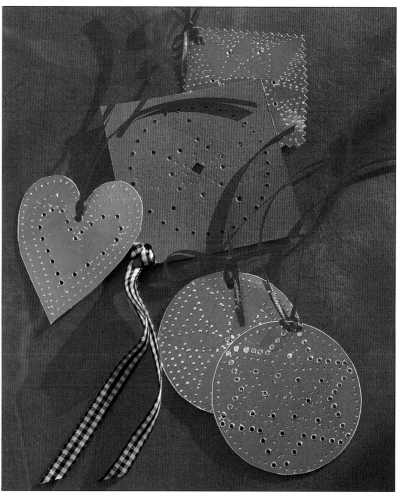

1 Cut out several different shapes from the metallic card (cardboard). Use a pair of compasses to draw the pinwheel pattern on the back of the card (cardboard).

2 Practise to get the feel of the pattern wheel, then, pressing evenly and firmly, use it to go over the pattern. Draw the other patterns in the same way.

3 Add a few strategically placed larger holes with the punch or a nail, then make a hole and thread with ribbon to complete the gift tag.

Paper Sculpture Rabbit

There is real magic in taking a flat sheet of paper and making it into something three dimensional. Paper sculpture involves accurate measuring, scoring, cutting and folding, which sounds like hard work, but is actually wonderfully absorbing.

This rabbit will make a delightful addition to any Easter gift, or you could make several to decorate an Easter egg tree. It could also be sent through the mail as an Easter greetings card.

YOU WILL NEED
tracing paper
pencil
stiff (heavy) paper
scissors
ruler
strand of raffia
double-sided adhesive
  (cellophane) tape

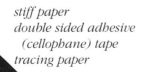
raffia

pencil  *scissors*

stiff paper
double sided adhesive
  (cellophane) tape
tracing paper

ruler

1 Trace the pattern on page 19 and enlarge it to the required size either on a photocopier or by squaring it up. Transfer the pattern on to stiff paper.

2 Cut out the shape, along all the solid lines.

3 Score along the dotted lines with the back of the scissors, then fold .

4 Fold up the rabbit and curl the tail around a pencil.

5 Poke two strands of raffia through for whiskers.

6 Place a small square of double-sided adhesive (cellophane) tape below the hole, peel off the backing and use this to secure the raffia and hold the head in position at the same time.

Edible Labels

These spice-cookie labels have the great advantage of wafting delicious smells around the house while they bake. A word of warning – tie them to the gifts at the last moment, lest the temptation to nibble is too great and the result is a pile of unnamed presents!

YOU WILL NEED
ready-mixed cookie dough
rolling pin
board
cookie cutters
ready-mixed icing
ribbon

cookie cutters

ready-mixed icing

ribbon

*cookie dough mixture
rolling pin
board*

COOK'S TIP
Remember to make a hole in your cookie labels before you bake them.

1 Roll out the dough to 1 cm (½ in) thick and cut out the cookies using different shaped cutters. Make holes for the ribbon (using a skewer is easiest). Bake in the oven at 180°C/350°F/Gas 4 for 10-12 minutes. Transfer to a wire rack to cool.

2 Decorate the cookies by piping on ready-mixed icing.

3 Thread the cookie labels with thin ribbon.

4 Tie red ribbon around the gift and secure the edible label, so that it lies flat on top of the parcel.

Elegant Embossed Cards

Embossed paper has a very subtle, expensive and specialist look about it, but is in fact not at all difficult to make. There are several different methods, but for a unique card or label the simplest way to do it is to place the paper over a stencil on a flat surface, and simply rub the back of the paper.

YOU WILL NEED
ready-cut stencil, or card (cardboard) cut-out
coloured paper, card (cardboard) and envelopes
embossing tool – blunt, smooth-ended plastic
scissors
PVA (white) glue

PVA (white) glue

scissors   *coloured paper*

paper

envelopes

embossing tool

stencil

1 Place the heart stencil (you will find it on page 19) on a flat work surface and cover it with the paper.

CRAFT TIP
You can cut a shape for embossing from thin cardboard. Experiment with different papers too, they all give different results. Remember that if it is too thin it will tear easily, so thicker paper is better.

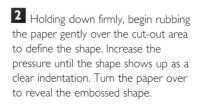

2 Holding down firmly, begin rubbing the paper gently over the cut-out area to define the shape. Increase the pressure until the shape shows up as a clear indentation. Turn the paper over to reveal the embossed shape.

3 Trim the paper to shape and stick it on to a red card (cardboard) background. Pair it up with a contrasting envelope or punch a hole in it, thread with ribbon and use it as a gift tag, if you wish.

Origami Gift Ornament

Origami is immensely popular, particularly with children, who seem to enjoy and understand the many complex folding instructions. As with paper sculpture, accurate folding is vital, but with origami there is no cutting or scoring, just a series of mountain and valley folds.

The gift here is wrapped using the principles of origami. The special folding and tucking means that you do not need to use tape to secure the parcel.

YOU WILL NEED
red origami paper
fine, handmade paper
scissors
PVA (white) glue

PVA (white) glue

scissors

red origami paper

handmade paper

1 To make the origami heart, take a square of red paper and fold two points across to meet each other on the centre line.

2 Then fold down the top corner to meet the bottom corner. Fold in half again, taking the right edge over to the left edge.

3 Fold the top corners over by 1 cm (½ in) and crease them.

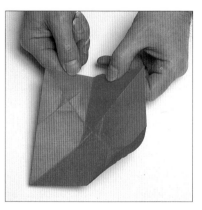

4 Open the shape out – it will have a diamond creased in the middle. Form a valley fold (inward) using the bottom edge of the diamond and extending the fold up to the top edge of the paper.

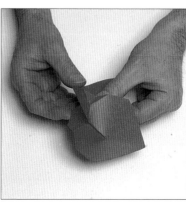

5 Fold over and tuck in the top two corners. The heart shape appears, raised up in the middle with the point facing downwards.

CRAFT TIP
To achieve really sharp paper folds, run the edge of your fingernail along the fold, pressing down firmly.

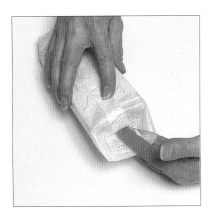

6 To wrap the parcel without tape, fold the top seam over in the usual way then tuck the folded side flap down and in, under the gift.

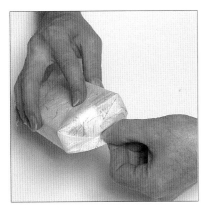

7 Bring the side flaps around, then tuck them with the bottom flap into the same place as the top flap. (Use a blunt instrument, like the round end of a pencil, to tuck all the paper away smoothly.) Position the heart on the gift using PVA (white) glue.

Message in a Bottle

This gift has a seaside theme, from the blue paper and shell decorations to the message in a bottle used as a gift tag. Private messages, love letters or poems can be written, folded and rolled up to fit into a small glass bottle, and if really secret, the cork can be secured with sealing wax!

YOU WILL NEED
small sheet of paper, for
  your message
gold pen
small corked glass bottle
sealing wax (for secrets)
cigarette lighter
raffia
sheet of sponged paper
double-sided adhesive
  (cellophane) tape
twisted paper ribbon
hot glue gun
shells or other seaside
  trimmings

twisted paper ribbon

hot glue gun

sealing wax
cigarette lighter

paper
gold pen

seaside trimmings

sponged paper

glass bottle

raffia

1 Write your message in gold pen, fold, roll up and fit it into the bottle.

2 Melt a small amount of sealing wax around the bottom of the cork and quickly push the cork into the bottle.

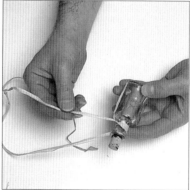

3 Loop the raffia around the neck and base of the bottle ready to tie on to the gift.

4 Wrap your gift in the sponged paper, securing it with double-sided tape. Untwist the paper ribbon and wrap in both directions around the parcel, gluing it underneath with the glue gun. Decorate the top of the ribbon with shells and other seaside trimmings. Finally, tie on the bottle.

Elegant Leaves

It is impossible to better Nature for shapes, textures and colours - so why try? Leaves make original and stylish gift tags, and look particularly good when teamed with rough handmade paper and garden raffia. Autumn is the prime time for leaf collecting, but freshly picked leaves can also be used, although the gift should be given on the same day, to avoid wilting.

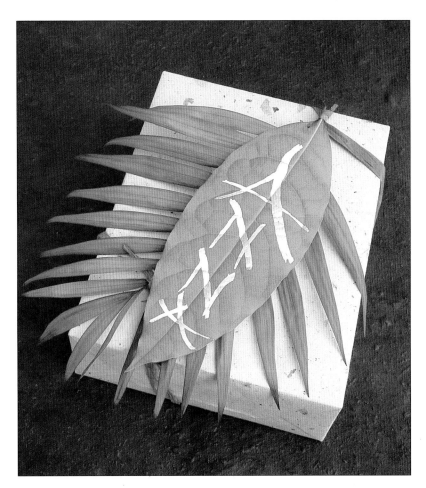

YOU WILL NEED
natural-coloured handmade paper
scissors
double-sided adhesive (cellophane) tape
suitable smooth-surfaced leaves
metallic felt-tipped pen
orange raffia

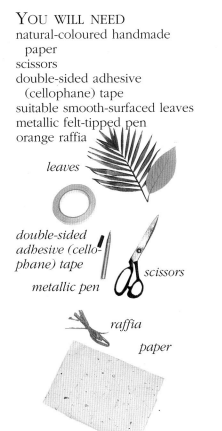

leaves

double-sided adhesive (cellophane) tape

metallic pen

scissors

raffia

paper

CRAFT TIP
This present has been given a hot tropical look by the use of palm and avocado pear tree leaves. The leaves are not brittle and can be easily secured with raffia and written on with metallic felt-tipped pen.

1 Cut the paper to fit your gift.

2 Wrap the present using double-sided tape. Select the leaves, leaving their stalks in place. The leaves should be perfectly shaped for the variety, with a smooth surface.

3 Test the flow of the pen on scrap paper, then write a name or message on the broadest leaf. Leave to dry for a few minutes.

4 Tie the leaves together and then on to the gift over opposite corners using orange raffia. Trim the raffia ends with scissors.

Valentine's Day Gift

A gift received on 14 February has only one meaning – love. It is an occasion that requires no restraint from the ardent gift-wrapper, so use all those ribbons, hearts, roses and bows to get your message across.

YOU WILL NEED
adhesive (cellophane)
  tape
heart-shaped cake base
scissors
red tissue paper
narrow ribbon
PVA (white) glue
white tissue paper
broader ribbon
drawing pin
white silk rose
tiny red satin flowers

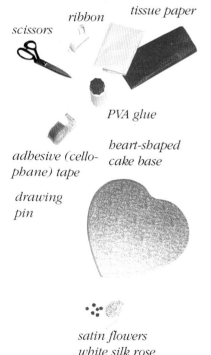

scissors   *ribbon*   *tissue paper*

PVA glue

adhesive (cello-phane) tape   *heart-shaped cake base*

drawing pin

satin flowers white silk rose

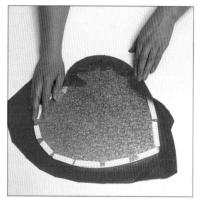

1 Apply double-sided adhesive (cellophane) tape around the outside edge of the underside of the cake base. Smooth out the red tissue paper, place heart face-down on to it and cut the paper to a large heart shape. Peel off the adhesive tape backing, one strip at a time, pull the paper up taut and stick it down. Continue around the heart. When you come to the dent, snip the paper to get a smooth fold.

CRAFT TIP

Heart-shaped boxes are difficult to find, but cake suppliers have covered cardboard cake bases made in heart shapes. The bases come in a range of sizes and although usually covered in shiny silver paper, this can be covered with red tissue paper. The beauty of this idea is that you can use it to wrap different shapes and still present them as heart-shaped.

2 To finish off the base, glue the narrow ribbon around the raised edge, and a paper heart across the back to cover the tissue paper edges.

4 Place the gift in the centre of the heart base. Cut four equal lengths of the broad ribbon, securing them through the centre point with a drawing pin in the middle of the heart's underside. Draw up the ribbons and tie them together at the centre of the gift.

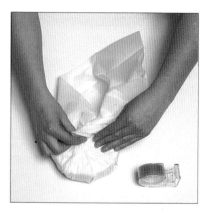

3 Wrap your gift in at least three layers of white tissue paper, securing the ends with adhesive (cellophane) tape.

5 Attach the white silk rose to cover the knot. If you like, tie a separate bow with the broad ribbon and position the rose at its centre. Decorate the edge of the gift with tiny red satin flowers, secured with glue.

Nest-egg

Easter is associated with rabbits, fluffy yellow chicks, spring flowers and, most deliciously, chocolate eggs. This project shows how to make a springtime nest from florist shop materials, to show off a traditional chocolate egg.

YOU WILL NEED
stiff cardboard
twisted willow wreath
scissors
hot glue gun
Easter themed ribbon
drawing pin
fake anenomes
dried moss
large chocolate egg
florist's wire

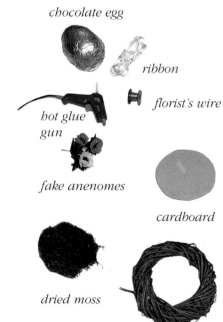

chocolate egg

ribbon

hot glue gun

florist's wire

fake anenomes

cardboard

dried moss

wreath

1 Cut a circle of cardboard to fit on the bottom of the willow wreath. Use a hot glue gun to stick it in place.

2 Cut two equal lengths of ribbon, long enough to secure to the cardboard base, pass round the egg and tie in a bow at the top. Use a drawing pin through the middle of the ribbons to attach them to the cardboard base. Thread each ribbon end through a twig of the wreath, as shown.

3 Poke the stems of the anenomes through the wreath, using the glue gun to secure them if necessary. Cut the moss to fit inside the wreath, forming a bed for the egg.

4 Place the egg in the nest, draw up the ribbons and tie them in a bow at the top.

5 Make an additional bow with extra ribbon using florist's wire (see pages 50 and 51) and secure it in place.

Birthday Treats

Here is a quick and easy way to make any gift look twice as exciting! The foil or crêpe paper is wrapped around the gift, then a long sheet of cellophane (plastic wrap) is wrapped around to cover it and gathered up at the ends like a giant candy. Twist and tie up with foil ribbon and add a small bag of real wrapped candies as a gift tag.

Just imagine waking up on your birthday to a pile of these at the end of your bed - it would be hard to believe that it wasn't just a dream.

YOU WILL NEED
bright crêpe paper (foiled or
  plain
scissors
adhesive (cellophane) tape
cellophane (plastic wrap)
  clear and coloured
foil ribbon
small bag of wrapped candies

1 Wrap your gift with the coloured crêpe paper, either foiled or plain.

2 Measure the length of your gift and cut the cellophane (plastic wrap) three times that length. Wrap around the gift and secure with tape.

3 Twist the ends and tie them close to the gift using foil ribbon.

4 Pull out the cellophane, trimming where necessary, to make a balanced candy shape. Attach a small bag of candies, or glue wrapped individual candies to the top of your gift.

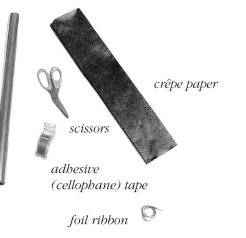

*cellophane
(plastic wrap)*

scissors

crêpe paper

*adhesive
(cellophane) tape*

foil ribbon

Wedding Present

The paper used here is dove grey overprinted with white Cupids, which gives a lovely damask effect. Instead of a ribbon, white net (tulle) has been gathered up into a big bow, like a bride's veil. The flowers are silk, and the effect is fresh and dramatic – this is a gift that will certainly stand out from all the rest!

YOU WILL NEED
1 sheet of dove grey handmade
  paper, depending on size
  of gift
Cupid rubber stamp
white watercolour paint and
  glass sheet
scissors
double-sided adhesive
  (cellophane) tape
thick white silk ribbon
1 m (3 ft) of white net (tulle)
florist's wire
small posy of white silk flowers

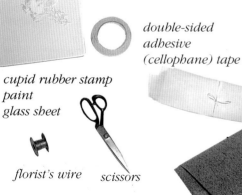

silk flowers

ribbon

*double-sided
adhesive
(cellophane) tape*

net (tulle)

*cupid rubber stamp
paint
glass sheet*

florist's wire   scissors

handmade paper

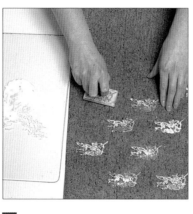

I Before wrapping it, place a gift card inside with the present – to avoid confusion! Now, randomly use the rubber stamp to print white Cupids all over the paper. Allow plenty of time for the paint to dry.

2 Place your gift in a box. Measure the paper allowing an excess of no more than 7.5 cm (3 in) as an overlap. Allow enough paper to fold the ends in neatly, but not so much as to appear bulky. Wrap up the box, securing the folded edges invisibly with double-sided tape. Run the ribbon around the box both ways and secure at the top with double-sided tape.

3 Divide the net (tulle) into two pieces. It will need to go twice around the box, so the amount used will depend upon the size. Tie the net (tulle) tightly each way around the box to meet at the centre at the top.

4 Make a big bow from two pieces of net (tulle). Use a generous amount for the body of the bow, gathering it up to make the loops and tails, but don't attempt to tie it. Use a small length of florist's wire, as shown on page 50, to hold the bow together in the middle. Now fold a short piece of net (tulle) three times into a flat sausage shape and fold this around the wire. Secure the ends with florist's wire and tuck under the bow.

5 Finally, finish the gift-wrap with a small posy of delicate silk flowers.

Golden Wedding Anniversary

Fifty years of marriage is an admirable achievement, so make sure that the happy couple feel suitably rewarded. When you are wrapping with gold, make it bold! There are different kinds of gold paper, the brightest is cellophane (plastic wrap) with a metallic coating on both sides. Matt antique gold paper has a dull gold sheen and is more muted in appearance.

YOU WILL NEED
1 sheet of gold wrapping paper, depending on size of gift
scissors
double-sided adhesive (cellophane) tape
broad gold ribbon
florist's wire
plastic pear and grapes
antique gold spray paint

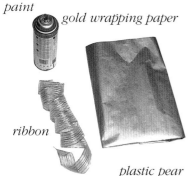

spray paint

gold wrapping paper

ribbon

plastic pear and grapes

scissors

florist's wire

double-sided adhesive (cellophane) tape

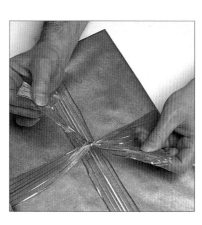

3 Cut a long length of ribbon and tie it around the box, crossing over underneath and tying firmly on the top. Trim off the ends.

CRAFT TIP
Try to find gold ribbon in a slightly deeper shade than the paper and choose trimmings that co-ordinate well. You can either spray the plastic fruit with antique gold aerosol, or use gilt cream, that is simply rubbed on to the surface and buffed when dry.

1 If your gift is not already boxed, find a box of a suitable size. Using the side of the box as a measuring guide, trim the paper to fit. You need no more than a 7.5 cm (3 in) overlap, and the ends should fold into neat triangles, with no bulky seams.

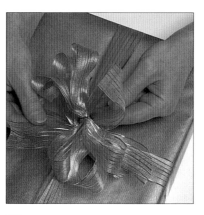

4 Make a large bow, securing the loops of ribbon in the centre with a binding of florist's wire, then cover the wire with a double thickness of ribbon, tying it loosely and tucking the ends under the bow, and using them to tie it to the box ribbons.

6 Attach the fruit to the top of the box by twisting florist's wire around the ribbon.

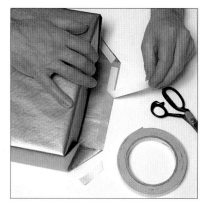

2 Use double-sided adhesive (cellophane) tape inside the top seam and at the centre points of the ends, to secure the paper invisibly.

5 Apply the gold spray to the fruit and, when dry, make up a bunch of the grapes and the pear.

Graduation Congratulations

The gift-wrapping used to wrap this bottle mimics the look of the certificate of qualification that has been earned, and ribbons and sealing wax are used for added dramatic effect.

YOU WILL NEED
corrugated packaging card
  board, 36 x 30 cm (14 x 12 in)
scissors
double-sided adhesive
  (cellophane) tape
tissue paper, plain and purple
sheet of vellum, parchment or
  similar paper
glass sheet
drop of cooking oil
sealing wax
cigarette lighter
broad gold ribbon
purple grosgrain ribbon
hot glue gun

*double-sided
adhesive (cello-
phane) tape*

*glass sheet
cooking oil
sealing wax
lighter*

hot glue gun

scissors

ribbons

*tissue paper
vellum
cardboard*

1 Roll up the bottle first in the corrugated cardboard, leaving about 2.5 cm (1 in) overhang at each end, and then the purple tissue. Secure with double-sided tape. Fill the spaces at the ends with scrunched-up tissue paper.

2 Make the seal on a sheet of oiled glass by lighting the wick and dripping into a 3 cm (1¼ in) diameter circle. Press a coin into it to make a patterned seal. Lift when cool.

3 Cut a length of broad gold ribbon and secure it around the parchment paper with double-sided tape. Cut a length of purple ribbon 45 cm (18 in) long and place it over the gold ribbon to cross at the join. Secure invisibly with double-sided tape.

4 Finally, add the red seal, using the glue gun, where the ribbons cross and trim back the ribbon tails to about 7.5 cm (3 in).

A Very Masculine Birthday Wrapping

This lizard-skin printed paper has a particularly male quality and the colour emphasizes this. It is perfect for wrapping a book or a shallow box. It is reminiscent of old leatherbound books and can be dressed up with a subtle matt ribbon, or be made more frivolous with contrasting bright green raffia.

YOU WILL NEED
sheet of lizard-skin effect printed paper
scissors
double-sided adhesive (cellophane) tape
green raffia

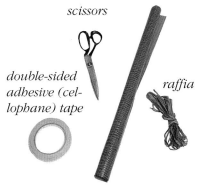

scissors

double-sided adhesive (cellophane) tape

raffia

lizard-skin effect printed paper

1 Place the gift on the paper and, allowing 4 cm (1½ in) overhang each end and three times the width, trim the paper down to size.

CRAFT TIP
Lizard-skin effect printed papers come in a range of colours and are available from specialist paper shops or craft shops.

2 Wrap the gift, folding in the ends and securing them invisibly with double-sided tape.

3 Take four strands of green raffia, and stretch and twist them together. Tie the raffia around the gift, crossing over underneath, then bringing up the ends and knotting at the centre point.

4 Tie the raffia into a bow, and trim the ends short.

House-warming Gift

A new house needs so many personal touches added before it looks and feels like home. This project uses a cardboard box to make a novelty gift container in the shape of a house.

YOU WILL NEED
strong cardboard box
scissors
sheet of rough-textured handmade paper, natural coloured
PVA (white) glue
sheet of corrugated cardboard
doll's-house roof-tile paper
narrow gingham ribbon

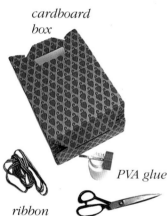

cardboard box

ribbon

PVA glue

scissors

corrugated card-board handmade paper doll's-house roof-tile paper

1 Find the centre point of the longest side flap of the box and draw lines to the sides, at least 7.5 cm (3 in) down from the top. Cut this triangular section away, and do the same to the other side. This gives you the pitch of the roof.

4 Measure the length of the roof along the line of the pitch, allowing a slight overlap at both sides. Cut the corrugated cardboard and roof-tile paper to the correct length and width and use PVA (white) glue to stick the two together.

2 Measure all around the box and cut the textured paper to fit. If your sheet is long enough you will be able to cut it out in one piece. Use the box itself as a pattern, turning it to draw out all the sides. Cut the paper out.

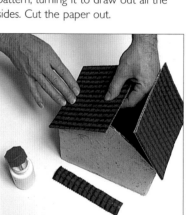

5 Cut the roof section in half, then glue each half to a side flap. The idea is to part the roof to open the box, so make sure that the two halves meet in the middle to form the point of the pitched roof. Cut a strip of cardboard roughly 4 cm (1½ in) wide and score it down the middle. Trim it to fit along the top of the roof, and cover with tile paper. It will sit on top of the roof and hold the two sides together, being held in place itself by the ribbon.

3 Spread the back of the textured paper with PVA (white) glue, right up to the edges, then smooth it in place over the box.

6 Pass a long length of gingham ribbon over the top of the roof, cross it over underneath the box and then pull it tight and tie it in a bow on top of the pitched roof.

Christmas Stripes

Christmas gift-wrap is produced in many thousands of variations, yet sometimes the most stylishly wrapped presents are relatively plain. This project is an example of how stripes of strong colour can be used on ordinary parcel wrap for a really dramatic effect.

CRAFT TIP
You can use a small decorating roller, as shown in the plaid paper project on pages 34 and 35, and the sponge versions can be cut in half to make a narrower stripe, if your gift is not large enough to show off the broad stripes. This project uses the roller full-size.

YOU WILL NEED
parcel wrap (packaging paper)
ruler
7.5 cm (3 in) decorator's rollers and tray (or small sponge brush, for smaller stripes)
dark green and white emulsion (latex) paint
saucers
scissors
double-sided adhesive (cellophane) tape
broad red moiré satin ribbon
florist's wire

parcel wrap (packaging paper)

florist's wire

double-sided adhesive (cellophane) tape

roller and tray

emulsion paint

ribbon

ruler

scissors

1 Lay a sheet of parcel wrap (packaging paper) on scrap paper. Use the roller to paint a white stripe, just in from the edge. Allow a roller's width plus 2 cm (¾ in), then paint the next white stripe. Repeat and leave to dry.

2 Use a fresh roller and the dark green paint. Begin painting the dark green stripe about 1.5 cm (½ in) away from the first white stripe, so that a small stripe of brown shows through. Repeat three times to complete the striped paper, and leave to dry.

3 Using the gift as a measuring guide, trim off any excess paper. Wrap the gift, securing the edges invisibly with double-sided tape.

4 Cut a long length of ribbon, taking it around the gift, crossing it underneath and tying it at the centre point on the top of the gift.

5 Make the bow by looping the ribbon over three times on each side and securing it with florist's wire.

6 Attach the bow to the parcel with an extra piece of ribbon.

Tower of Boxes

It is always a good idea to save boxes throughout the year as they make gift-wrapping such a pleasure. Here is an idea for presenting three separate gifts, or perhaps one that consists of three different parts. Each gift or component is placed in a different sized box, and then they are tied up in a stack with bright plaid ribbon.

YOU WILL NEED
range of different sized boxes –
  minimum number three
3 sheets of identical plain-
  coloured paper
scissors
double-sided adhesive
  (cellophane) tape
plaid ribbon
florist's wire

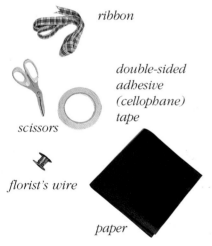

ribbon

double-sided adhesive (cellophane) tape

scissors

florist's wire

paper

VARIATION
Naturally, there is no need to stop at three boxes, you could continue stacking boxes of diminishing size if you have gifts to fill them. As a variation, you could use three different bright-coloured tissue papers to wrap the boxes, and gold ribbon and tassels to tie them.

1 Using the boxes as a measuring guide, trim the paper down to avoid any bulky folds.

2 Wrap each box, using double-sided adhesive (cellophane) tape inside the folds to secure the paper invisibly.

3 Use the height of the box stack to estimate the length of ribbon required. It will be roughly five times the height. Find the middle of the ribbon length and place it in the centre of the top box, then take the ends down to cross underneath and tie up on the top.

4 Make a three-looped bow, twisting the centre together with florist's wire, then tie a piece of ribbon over the bow and on to the top of the box. Pull out the loops of the bow and trim the ribbon ends into V shapes.

Bold Red and Gold

There is something sumptuous about red tissue paper – the rustling noise and smooth texture seem to impart a sense of luxury, and the colour deepens with layering. Stamp the paper with large gold stars and you will have one of the most stunning gift-wraps around.

YOU WILL NEED
pack of red tissue paper
big star rubber stamp
gold ink
saucer
adhesive (cellophane) tape
scissors
gold ribbon, cord or tinsel

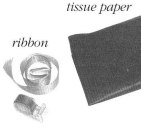

tissue paper

ribbon

adhesive (cellophane) tape

gold ink

scissors

rubber stamp

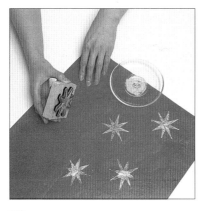

1 Lay a sheet of tissue paper on to scrap paper and, beginning in one corner, work diagonally across the sheet, stamping stars about 5 cm (2 in) apart. Leave to dry.

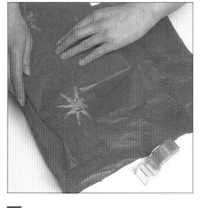

2 Wrap the gift using a lining of one or two sheets of plain red tissue paper under the stamped sheet. Use adhesive tape to secure the ends. (If desired, use double-sided adhesive (cellophane) tape for invisible joins.)

3 Trim the gift with a gold ribbon tied on top with a single bow.

4 Swallowtail the ribbon ends for a professional finish.

Season's Greetings – the Natural Look

This project will appeal to those who feel a sense of visual indigestion when faced with all the glitz of Christmas.

A sheet of plain brown parcel wrap (packaging paper) is folded around the gift, then a light airy collage of festive tissue paper shapes is applied. The gift is tied up with coarse brown string and decorated with cones and pods.

YOU WILL NEED
parcel wrap (packaging paper)
scissors
double-sided adhesive
  (cellophane) tape
pencil
tracing paper
white chalk
dark blue and orange tissue
  paper
PVA (white) glue
thick coarse string
selection of dried cones and
  pods
hot glue gun

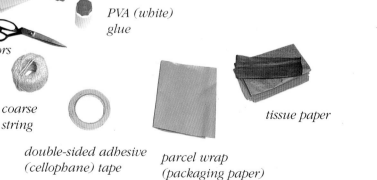

tracing paper

hot glue gun

cones and pods

PVA (white) glue

scissors

coarse string

double-sided adhesive (cellophane) tape

parcel wrap (packaging paper)

tissue paper

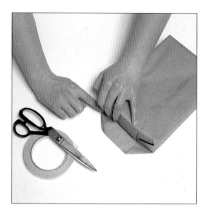

1 Use the box as a measuring guide and cut the parcel wrap to size.

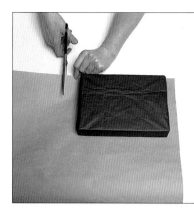

2 Wrap the box using double-sided adhesive (cellophane) tape.

3 Trace the shapes on page 21 and cut them out of blue and orange tissue paper. You will need to use chalk to transfer the shapes on to the darker paper. The number you will need depends upon the size of your gift.

4 Experiment with the positioning of the shapes until you are happy with the arrangement, then apply a thin layer of glue, spread with your finger, directly on to the paper. Quickly smooth the tissue shapes on to the glue.

5 Tie coarse string around the gift, crossing it over underneath and knotting it on top. Untwist the string ends and fluff them out, then trim neatly.

6 Use the glue gun to stick a small arrangement of miniature cones and pods to the knotted string.

The Ice Box

A great big box under the Christmas tree always attracts attention, but this stunning present is in danger of upstaging the Christmas tree itself!

The blue paper is stencilled with snowflakes, then the whole gift is bunched up in clear icy cellophane (plastic wrap). Foil ribbons and Christmas tree ornaments complete the effect.

YOU WILL NEED
tracing paper
pencil
cardboard or mylar
craft knife
bright blue paper
small sponge
bowl of water
white watercolour paint
saucer
adhesive (cellophane) tape
scissors
roll of clear, wide cellophane
  (plastic wrap)
silver foil ribbon
selection of Christmas tree
  ornaments

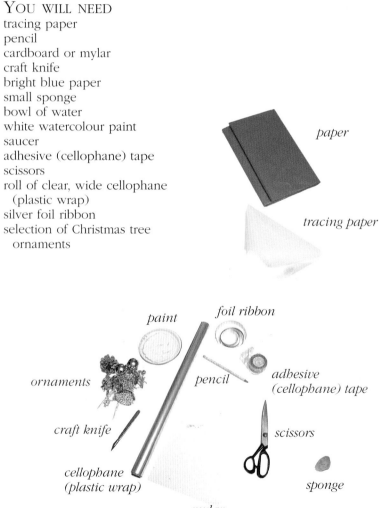

paper

tracing paper

paint *foil ribbon*

ornaments *pencil* *adhesive (cellophane) tape*

craft knife *scissors*

cellophane (plastic wrap) *sponge*

mylar

1 Trace and cut out the stencil on page 20. You can use cereal box cardboard or special stencil plastic called mylar. Take care when using the craft knife.

3 If one sheet of paper is not big enough to cover the box, lay two sheets side by side and run a length of adhesive (cellophane) tape along the join. Repeat with other sheets until you have a single sheet large enough for the box. Wrap up the box, using adhesive (cellophane) tape to hold the wrapping securely in place.

2 Place scrap paper on your work surface and use a small sponge to apply the white paint. Dip the sponge in the bowl of water then squeeze it out thoroughly. Stencil paints should always be on the dry side to prevent any from seeping under the stencil. Apply the snowflakes randomly all over the blue paper and right over the edges. Allow to dry thoroughly.

4 Unroll a length of cellophane (plastic wrap) on your work surface long enough to pass under the box, up the sides and allowing at least 30 cm (12 in) extra on both ends. Do the same in the other direction, to cross over the first sheet under the box.

CRAFT TIP

This gift-wrap really works best on a large scale, so if you have a boxed toy, stereo or television to wrap, look no further.

5 Gather up the cellophane (plastic wrap) on top of the box, making sure that the sides of the box are completely covered, then tape around the bunch, close to the box top.

6 Cover the adhesive (cellophane) tape with silver foil ribbon and attach the Christmas tree decorations.

Christmas Balls

Plain Christmas tree balls can be transformed into totally unique decorations. Customize the balls by adding surface decorations with a hot glue gun – ribbons, sequins, fake gemstones, eyelets, glitter glue and fabric paints, for example.

YOU WILL NEED
red and gold balls
hot glue gun
decorations – sequins, gem
  stones, glitter glue, metallic
  stars
tweezers
fancy gold cord
scissors

hot glue
gun

balls

decorations

tweezers

cord

scissors

1 Draw stripes of glue down the red ball with the glue gun to divide it into quarters. Sprinkle it immediately with sequins.

2 Place a dot of glue in the middle of each panel and stick on a metallic star.

3 Stick the gemstones around the gold ball with the glue gun. Position them with the tweezers.

4 Surround each gemstone with a setting of glitter glue. Finally, thread all the balls with gold cord, and tie them on to gifts or a Christmas tree.

Gingham and String Wreath

This little wreath will look pretty on a gingham or plain wrapped parcel. It could hang up in the kitchen or on the Christmas tree - or even on the doll's house front door!

YOU WILL NEED
ruler
thick, coarse string
scissors
hot glue gun
2.5 cm (1 in) red gingham ribbon
narrow black gingham ribbon
small dried cone
very narrow black satin ribbon

hot glue gun

cone

scissors

ribbons

ruler

string

1 Cut three 18 cm (7 in) lengths of string. Use the glue gun to draw a line down one piece, then roll a length of red gingham ribbon around it. You may need a few extra dabs for a smooth covering.

2 Glue the three string ends together, with the gingham one in the middle.

3 Hold the gingham still and cross the other strings over in front and behind it, along its length, then glue the three ends together. Form the braid into a ring shape and glue the two ends together. Hold the join until the glue cools and sets (it takes seconds).

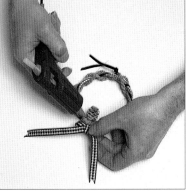

4 Tie a bow with the black gingham ribbon. Add one more dab of glue and stick the cone and gingham bow in place. Finally, weave the black ribbon through the wreath to tie at the top.

Paper Sculpture Birds

These birds have a bright, crisp contemporary feel, with a touch of folk art in the painting. They look great on gifts, and several of them strung on nylon make a fabulous mobile. Imagine a Christmas tree covered with these bright, colourful little birds – a project for all the family.

YOU WILL NEED
pencil
tracing paper
stiff (heavy) coloured paper
scissors
ruler
stapler
hole punch
paints
saucers
paintbrush
fine cord

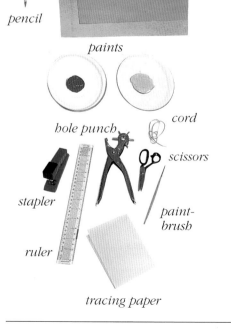

stiff (heavy) paper

pencil

paints

cord

hole punch

scissors

stapler

paint-brush

ruler

tracing paper

3 Use the blunt edge of the scissors to score fold lines at 0.5 cm (¼ in) intervals across the wings, then pleat them.

1 Trace the pattern on page 18 then transfer it to the coloured papers.

2 Cut out the bird body and wing shapes.

4 Staple a wing to each half of the bird and fan the wings out. Punch a small hole through both sides for the bird's eyes.

5 Paint spots on the underside of the bird bodies and when dry add a small contrasting spot in the middle of each.

6 Punch a hole through the top of the bird, about halfway along, and thread it through with fine cord.

Spice Decoration

Cinnamon sticks keep their rich, spicy smell for many many years, and provide a perfect base to which other natural decorations can be added. Use any combination of ribbons, lace, fine chain, gold cord and bells along with cones, grasses and seed pods.

YOU WILL NEED
long cinnamon sticks
hot glue gun
selection of bark, cones, seed pods and dried foliage
narrow red ribbon
gold cord
small bell

natural decorations

cones
dried foliage
cinnamon sticks

ribbon

hot glue gun

cord

1 Join the cinnamon sticks together to make a staggered raft shape. Use the glue gun to make this base.

2 Stick individual natural decorations on to the base with dabs of hot glue from the glue gun.

3 Wrap the ribbon around the bundle, crossing it over several times before tying it at the back.

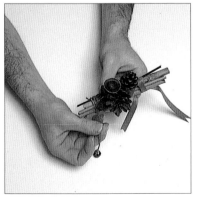

4 Wind the gold cord around the decoration, tie the bell to the end of the cord, and leave the end with the bell dangling down.

Folded Star

A glorious starburst is hard to beat as a Christmas decoration. It symbolizes the Star of Bethlehem suspended in the dark night sky, and the glossy black paper used on this gift shows the star off in a similar way. The star is made from three folded paper stars, placed on top of each other for a three-dimensional effect.

YOU WILL NEED
pencil
tracing paper
scalpel
stiff (heavy) yellow paper
pair of compasses
ruler
PVA (white) glue

tracing paper

paper *scalpel*

PVA (white) glue

ruler

compasses and pencil

VARIATION
The stars also look great hanging up. Just use a needle and thread through one of the points and suspend them in front of a window or on the Christmas tree.

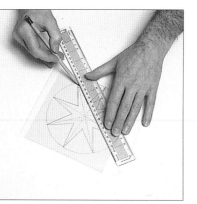

1 Trace the pattern on page 18 and draw out three stars on to the yellow paper. Cut out the shapes with a scalpel to ensure a clean edge. (Enlarge the pattern if preferred.)

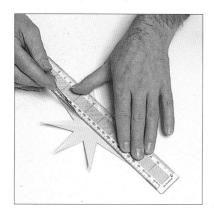

2 The star is made by alternate mountain and valley folds. Score all the fold lines with the back of the scalpel against a ruler.

3 Fold up the stars, sharpening the creases between your finger and thumbnail.

4 Arrange the stars behind one another, adding a tiny dab of glue to each centre. If you are using the star flat on a gift, then press it gently on to a small piece of double-sided adhesive (cellophane) tape.

ACKNOWLEDGEMENTS

The Publishers would like to
thank the following companies
for supplying materials used in
this book:

Offray Ribbons for supplying
all the ribbons used in this
book. Fir Tree Place, Church
Road, Ashford, Middlesex,
TW15 2PH. Tel: 01734 732888.

Paint Magic for Paintability
Stencil for Spring Meadow
Stencil, p 24. 79 Shepperton
Road, Islington, London N1
3DF. Tel: 0171 354 9696.

The Blue Cat Toy Company
for Fishy Imprints, p 25.
Builders Yard, Silver Street,
South Cerney, Gloucestershire,
GL7 5TS. Tel: 01285 861 867